- Establish a good relationship with students and their families
- Get the most out of limited resources
- Learn the ins and outs of administration and build rapport with other teachers

Melissa Kelly

Published by
Adams Media, a division of F+W Media, Inc.
57 Littlefield Street, Avon, MA 02322. U.S.A.
www.adamsmedia.com

ISBN-10: 1-59869-656-4
ISBN-13: 978-1-59869-656-1

Printed in the United States of America.

10 9 8 7 6 5 4 3

Library of Congress Cataloging-in-Publication Data
is available from the publisher.

Contains material adopted and abridged from *The Everything® New Teacher Book* by Melissa Kelly, Copyright © 2004 by F+W Publications, Inc.

This book is available at quantity discounts for bulk purchases.
For information, please call 1-800-289-0963.

Contents

Introduction

Your Personal Mentor

Teaching is a fascinating and at the same time extremely complicated profession. As a teacher, you will have the opportunity to affect the lives of thousands of young people. Think back to your elementary, middle, and high school days. Are there teachers that you still fondly remember? Did one or more profoundly change the way you look at life? Are there some who had a negative impact on you? Just answering these questions will help you see the impact you will have on those you teach.

The prospect of teaching students and having such an effect on their future can seem scary. The goal of this book is to give you practical tips and sources of inspiration to guide you on your rewarding career in education. Look at it as your mentor that you can turn to while you work through some of the major issues you will be facing as you teach. While no book can replace actual teaching experience, the strategies and guides presented here will alleviate some of the concerns you have while making your life easier and your time teaching more productive.

You will hear a lot of discussion about the troubles facing the state of education in the United States today. While there are a lot of improvements that can be made in the realm of education, there is also a lot of good that is occurring each day in classrooms across the nation. Trite though it might sound, the solution can really begin with you, one class and one student at a time.

Part One

Growing the Teacher Within

Teaching is a unique profession in that there is not one right way to teach a class of students. In fact, if you compared two effective teachers you would probably find that they differed from each other in many ways. Yet, at their core these effective teachers share certain key skills that they use to help their students learn and grow. Recognizing and cultivating these skills will help you grow as an educator while increasing your connection with your students.

1 Face Your New Reality

Effective teachers are truly dedicated professionals. A teacher's day typically starts early and ends late. Your day will probably begin with some planning time that allows you to make last-minute preparations for the students. Once the students arrive in the classroom, you cannot expect another moment of quiet until your next planning period or the end of the day.

Each class is a new challenge. You will find some students who love learning and some who despise it. You will present your lesson and hopefully not have more than one or two unexpected disruptions such as fire drills, announcements, unexpected visitors, and the dreaded student disruptions. Hopefully, you will also experience one or more moments that will help you remember why you became a teacher. When the day ends, you will probably have meetings to attend before you can settle down to some grading and planning for the next day. Many teachers take home grading each evening. Through all of this, it's important to remember throughout each day to keep a sense of humor and remember that you are truly affecting future generations.

2 Anticipate Your Students' Expectations

All people want to succeed, even if they fear success. Many students realize that they could have done a better job in their last school year. Maybe they didn't spend enough time doing homework, or perhaps they never found time to read their texts. The new school year is the perfect time to turn over a new leaf and start fresh.

Students Are as Nervous as You

Remember the last time you were in a new classroom with a teacher you had never met? Even if you had a friend or two in the class, there was most probably an element of nervousness in the air. Many of your students will feel the same.

Students will show their nervousness in a variety of ways. Most of them will probably be very quiet. Even if you try to make a joke, you might not get a lot of response. It will take some coaxing to get students out of their shells. Learning students' names quickly can help them feel more welcome and relaxed.

A few students will come into your class on the first day with a chip on their shoulders. This too is a sign of nervousness. These students don't feel comfortable, so they become defensive. Just knowing this can help you make better decisions on how to react to a student's misbehavior realizing that this is not necessarily an indication of future behavioral problems. At this point, humor is the biggest tool you have in your teaching arsenal.

3 Learn the Ingredients for Success

What makes a teacher successful? Many people feel that a successful teacher is someone who is well organized and has detailed lesson plans. While many effective teachers do share these habits, they are not enough. In fact, some successful teachers are very unorganized in teaching and other areas of their lives. This does not mean that organization is not important for them too; it would make their lives easier if they were better organized and planned more detailed lessons. But this does not take away from the fact that they are effective as teachers.

So if organization and detailed lesson plans are not enough, what qualities do successful teachers possess? The ingredients for success include the following:

- Sense of fairness
- Consistent approach
- Ability to be flexible
- Positive attitude
- High expectations for yourself and your students
- Sense of humor

The first three of these are skills you practice each day. The second three should become part of your overall personality. All of these characteristics can be achieved through experience and practice. The strategies in this book will help make these attributes a part of your effective teaching repertoire.

Keep a Positive Attitude

Every day, you set the tone in the classroom with your attitude. You are on stage from the moment your students arrive until they rush back out the door to their next class. If you have a negative attitude, your students will also adopt this mindset, and your class will most probably not be very productive. On the other hand, if you have a positive attitude toward your students, your subject, your profession, and yourself, you will find that this optimism pervades the class. You will probably have a much more productive and enjoyable day.

The effects of a positive attitude have been widely studied. They include the following:

- Improved job satisfaction
- Better self-esteem
- Improved personal interactions
- Better health
- Greater achievement levels
- Improved overall happiness

Everyone has experienced what it's like to be around a negative person. They usually wind up ruining the whole day. Just think how your students are going to feel after spending time with you if you are pessimistic about them or your curriculum. Some days will be harder than others but the benefits of being positive make it all worthwhile.

5 Be Consistent

Consistency in teaching basically means that your students know what to expect from you day to day. Your rules do not change. You are not strict one day and easygoing the next. There are no surprises for your kids, and they do not have to feel like they are walking on eggshells. Consistency is important if you want to earn the respect of your students.

If you spend some time in a consistent teacher's classroom, you will find that every student knows the rules. Students know what is expected of them, and there is no question of what will happen if they fail to live up to those expectations. The teacher's demeanor in a consistent classroom does not change from period to period or day to day. Because everyone knows the consequences, and there is no doubt about the reaction of the teacher, misbehavior is greatly reduced. Students in a consistent classroom can feel safe and can focus on what is important—not what mood the teacher happens to be in on a particular day. This is one of the main secrets that effective teachers share.

Make Sure to Follow Through

Another important aspect of consistency is following through. If you tell your students that you are going to do something, then you had better do it or they will lose respect for you. It is very important that you do not threaten your students with actions that you will not or cannot take.

Let's say your class is misbehaving during a quiz, and that some students are being particularly disruptive. You threaten the class that everyone is in danger of getting a zero. This is a good example of an idle threat. Realistically, it is not something you should or even would do. For one thing, your administration might have a real problem with this action, especially after parents begin calling. Plus, there are probably some good students in the class who are not being disruptive, and punishment would be completely unfair to them.

A Day-to-Day Practice

You will have bad days as a teacher. But even if you're having a bad day, you should try to be consistent in your actions and reactions. In fact, these days are the measure of your consistency.

Obviously, you will have moments when you react in a manner that is not truly consistent. You might lash out at a talkative student on a day you have a bad headache. But the less frequent these instances are, the more your students will respect you and the more effective you will be.

Learn to Be Fair

It is hard to determine whether consistency or fairness is the more important skill for a teacher. Students do not respect inconsistent teachers. However, they have a real problem with teachers they perceive as unfair. If you think back to your time as a student, you can probably remember at least one teacher you or your fellow students thought was unfair. This might have been someone who favored a certain group of students or someone whose rules seemed almost arbitrary. In the end, this teacher probably lost the respect of most students.

It is possible to train yourself to be fairer as a teacher. Take stock of your actions at the end of each day to see where you might not have acted fairly. Give yourself time before making decisions concerning discipline in your classroom. Sometimes giving the disruptive student and yourself a cooling-off period will allow you to approach the situation more rationally. Everyone makes mistakes, and no one is fair all the time. However, students will notice and appreciate your attempts to treat all students equally and with an equal measure of respect every day.

Start Each Day Fresh 8

Fairness pervades your classroom environment. Students are very perceptive at telling how fair you really are as a teacher based on your daily actions. If you consistently enforce rules in the same manner for all students, then you will be perceived as fair.

Are there situations in which you want to act in a manner that might be seen as unfair? Sure there are. It can be very tough to enforce a rule when the student breaking it is normally excellent. Built into your discipline system should be levels of offenses. In other words, as a student breaks a rule more times, the punishment should change. This will help you in your effort to be fair. The student who makes one mistake will not be punished the same as the one who makes many.

It can also be very difficult to act fairly to a student who is normally disruptive. However, experience proves that if you treat each day as a clean slate in terms of your reactions to the students, you will find that their behavior will not be quite as extreme. If there are students who are perpetually in trouble, they will expect you to treat them more harshly, thus giving them no incentive to try and act better. If you surprise them by not holding grudges, you in turn may be pleasantly surprised by the results. This does not mean that students should go unpunished for their offenses. It just means that you need to watch your actions and attitude when approaching these students each day.

9 Be Flexible

Flexibility in teaching as in yoga is an important skill. Both students and teachers are happier at school and in their future life if they can learn to adjust to changing environments and situations.

For example, say you have created a multipart lesson plan that allows for five minutes of warm-up time, twenty minutes of class discussion, twenty minutes of small group discussion, and five minutes of end-of-the-period review. However, once the whole group discussion actually begins, the students get really involved. They are enjoying the conversation, and there's a lot of learning and interchange of ideas going on. Do you decide at this point to cut the discussion short to follow your schedule? Or do you allow the discussion to continue so as not to lose momentum?

Obviously, you would want to allow the discussion to continue. Moments like this can be rare, and they are wonderful to behold when they happen. It is your job as a teacher to capitalize on your class's excitement and not be hemmed in by a lesson plan you wrote the week before.

Keep Your Expectations High

10

As educators, it is important to change the perception that high expectations set students up to fail. They don't—but low or impossible expectations do. Low expectations can create a false sense of accomplishment that is not based on reality. If your class is extremely easy, you will not be preparing students for future, more rigorous classes. Students will not have a true sense of what it takes to succeed. High expectations, however, can lead to authentic and heightened self-esteem.

Students need to feel that you believe they can do it, that they can learn. Having high expectations does not mean that a student is a failure if he does not understand a subject or has a hard time with it. It simply means that you expect him to try, and that with additional help, you believe he can do it. This is definitely not a recipe for failure. Instead, students who have never been respected academically will probably begin acknowledging your efforts through their words and actions. If reinforced enough, they will begin to believe that they can succeed.

11 Shed Those Biases

Most biases are based on your past experiences and beliefs. Some of them are even based on your own fears about your abilities. In education, it is important to face your biases and determine whether they are valid as beliefs. Here are some of the more predominant biased beliefs:

- Some students just cannot (or will not) learn.
- A good teacher must teach to the lowest/middle/highest student.
- Some information is too difficult.
- AP students do not need extra help.

Any of these biases is enough to produce negative expectations and results, both in your professional life and in the life of your students. It is impossible to have high expectations for your students if you don't believe that they can achieve in your class. You must keep alive the belief that students can learn what you are teaching them or you will doom them to fail.

Be careful to examine your biases. Even if you think that they are hidden, your actions will reveal what you truly believe. Students will be able to pick up on your negative opinions, which could seriously limit the learning environment.

12 9 Methods to Communicate Expectations

Here are nine methods you might use to let your students know your expectations:

1. Get students to sign an "Achievement Contract" outlining what you expect of them and what they should expect from you.
2. Give students enough time to find answers on their own, providing only hints and ideas.
3. Periodically allow students to express how they think they are doing in the course.
4. Speak to students in a positive manner at all times, stressing that you know they have the ability to learn what you are teaching.
5. Try to get to know your students and allow them to see you as a real person; this will motivate some of your students to work harder in order to please you.
6. Remain in charge of your students as their teacher, and don't try to be their friend.
7. Make your standards for assignments and activities absolutely clear by telling students exactly what you expect from them.
8. Make sure you let all students know that they can earn an A in your course if they work hard enough.
9. Promote mastery learning by allowing students to revise assignments that received low grades.

13 Learn How Students Respond to Goals

Student misbehavior is one of the biggest fears of new and inexperienced teachers. New teachers are unsure of what to expect. However, if you go into the classroom expecting a high level of cooperation and behavior, you will have a better shot at achieving your goals. Approaching a classroom with fear and the belief that students will misbehave becomes a self-fulfilling prophecy. Those teachers who approach student behavior in a positive manner—without believing kids will always misbehave—are the teachers who have better classroom management skills and lower stress levels.

Their Grades Might Go Up!

If you let students know that you believe they can get an A in your class, they already have one person in their corner. By constantly reinforcing the idea that you think each student can get good grades, you are helping them believe in themselves. Now, not all students will earn As in your classroom, but many of them will make a greater effort to do better than they have previously.

One idea that works for some teachers is allowing students to redo assignments that receive a low grade, like 80 percent or lower. Establish strict rules concerning the procedure and the deadline for resubmitting the assignment. Yes, this does mean more work for you, but over time many students will turn in better work the first time as they fully understand what you expect of them.

14 Accomplish Your Own Goals

Setting high (not impossible!) expectations for yourself is important in setting yourself up to achieve your goals. We can't ever succeed if we start out believing we have lost. You can only succeed in teaching and other areas of life if you believe that you can do it. It is a good idea to frequently reflect on areas where you need to improve in your teaching. Set goals for yourself, and track your progress over time. Continually tweak what you are doing to refine your teaching skills.

The benefits of defining your expectations are many. First, you will find that you are less stressed because you will have a better understanding of what is important to you. While you will still face stresses in the job, you will be able to approach them with firm values and beliefs in place. Second, your attitude will definitely improve. You will be more positive about what you and others can achieve. Finally, your confidence level will rise. If you believe that you too can learn and achieve, then you will begin accomplishing your goals.

15 Develop a Vision

The role of teachers has expanded to a point that it is sometimes difficult to grasp exactly what is expected. Today, education is the topic of many social and political debates. The problems that education faces are not clear-cut, and the answers to these problems are even less apparent. In this atmosphere of blame and reform, teachers often find themselves sinking instead of soaring. To keep your sanity, you must define the role you are going to have in education as part of your expectations and goals.

Teaching has become much more complicated over time. Teachers wear many hats:

- Facilitator
- Surrogate parent
- Coach
- Record keeper
- Nurse
- Guidance counselor
- Knowledge specialist
- Technology expert
- Special-education expert
- Social worker

The truth is that no one person can fulfill all of these roles. It is your job as a teacher to decide where to put your emphasis. Develop a clear vision of the role you want to play. This will give you the power to make a much greater impact and will also shield you from the pressures and stresses that affect many other teachers.

16 Don't Be Afraid to Succeed!

You can be a success as a teacher with effort and common sense. It is a fact that many teachers quit teaching within the first three years. If you truly feel that teaching is your life's work then don't become another teacher who gives up before they've even begun. Instead, work hard to improve your skills. If you feel like you need it, ask fellow effective teachers who you trust to come observe your class during their planning period to give you advice. They might be able to give you specific suggestions that could make all the difference.

Teaching can seem a scary endeavor. However, even if you do not feel confident when you walk into your classroom, you need to follow the old adage and "fake it until you make it." In other words, pretend that you are confident, and eventually you will gain confidence. Once you have mastered the technical aspects of teaching, such as paperwork, discipline, and lesson plans, you can really begin to reap the benefits. You will find that teaching is a very worthwhile and rewarding endeavor.

17 If You Make a Mistake . . .

All teachers, even those who are truly effective, make mistakes. You will have times when your attitude is bad no matter what you do, or when you are inconsistent, unfair, or inflexible despite yourself. These can become learning opportunities if you handle them the right way. It is not wrong or a sign of weakness to admit that you made a mistake or to apologize to your students. Once the incident is over, move on with a renewed commitment to avoid that mistake again. Teachers who act as if an obvious mistake on their part was not wrong will lose their student's respect.

The best teachers are the best learners. Allow yourself the opportunity to learn as you teach. We learn from books, certainly, but our everyday lives in the classroom also offer lessons on personal and professional growth. Mistakes allow us to grow. If we did everything right the first time, we would never have anything to learn. Mistakes are opportunities that can become our springboards to newer heights.

18 Develop a Teaching Style All Your Own

No two teachers are alike, just as no two people are alike. Teachers come from different backgrounds, and they have educational memories and experiences that shape their attitudes about teaching. Realize that your memories of how your own instructors taught may not work for you or even be sound educational practice.

It is fine to work with mentors and to emulate some of their best qualities. However, you will be happiest and most successful if you take the information presented here and combine it with the advice of experienced, effective teachers to create your own teaching style. Look for positive teaching skills in each teacher you meet, and include them in your own practices.

Try to approach every day as a new opportunity to grow and achieve your goals. Above all, try to have fun. Teaching should not be drudgery but should be full of exciting opportunities for sharing and growth. When you wake up each morning excited to go to work, you will be more satisfied and more effective.

Part Two

Classroom Management 101

Before you begin your first day, you should have systems in place to deal with the housekeeping issues that will arise. This is the beginning of effective classroom management. If you have to devise these once the school year has begun, you will be playing catch-up for the rest of the year. This section will help you to get organized and to create some tools that will better prepare you to deal with behavioral issues that may arise in your class.

19 Get Your Rules Straight

Some common mistakes that new teachers make when they create rules are creating too many and making them too general. Your goal should be to aim for five good, specific rules. This will make your life much easier as the year goes on. Rules that are too general are typically harder to enforce.

Following are some other examples of rules that you could choose from to use in your class:

- Be in your seat when the bell rings.
- Follow directions the first time they are given.
- Raise your hand and wait until you are recognized before speaking.
- Stay in your assigned seat unless otherwise stated.
- No cursing or vulgar or offensive language.
- Keep your desk and surrounding area clean.
- Eyes front when the teacher is talking.
- Come to class with all books and necessary materials.
- No personal grooming in class.
- Respect others by not talking while others are speaking.

As you can see, there are more than five listed here. Some of these are aimed at younger students and some at older. Choose what is best for your situation.

Enforce Rules from Day One

20

How should you present your rules to students? The simplest method is to simply post your rules in your room before the first day of school. They should be in dark, permanent marker on a poster board that is visible to all students. When students come in the first day and you are orienting them for the year, refer to the chart on the wall and go through each rule. Every time someone violates a rule, refer again to the chart as you explain what the student did wrong.

Another approach that some teachers take is to have the students involved in creating the class rules, thereby creating a sense of buy-in for the students. This approach can be extremely effective as long as you feel confident in your ability to control the focus and direction of the discussion.

It is important that students know and learn your class rules, but it is also essential to inform the parents. A good habit is to send home a copy of your classroom rules for parents to sign. When parents are informed, fewer misunderstandings will occur.

21 Make Rules Apply to Everyone, Every Day

As a consistent, effective teacher, it is important to emphasize that your rules are the same every day for all students. If your rules are not specific and are difficult to enforce, this could be a problem. By maintaining a consistent message about the rules, you are more likely to enforce them, and students are more likely to follow them.

Some teachers start with good intentions by creating specific class rules. However, these same teachers often fail to enforce the rules consistently. You'll recognize their classes as soon as you walk into one—by the chaos within. Students will pick up on any weakness related to rule enforcement on your part. This is especially important in the beginning of the year when students are getting used to you and your class. As the year goes on, if things are going well you might be able to loosen up somewhat. But remember, it is always easier to get easier.

What if you find that a rule is not working or that another rule is necessary? As the teacher, you can replace a rule if the need arises. If you have created the proper climate of consistency and fairness, the transition to a new and necessary rule should be relatively painless.

Make Do with Missing School Supplies 22

Each day you will have students who come to class unprepared. They might have left their book at home or simply have no paper or pencil. The question that you face as a teacher is the method in which you deal with this situation.

Two major schools of thought seem to exist on this issue. One is that students need to learn to be responsible. Therefore, if they do not come prepared, they should not be able to participate in the lesson or they should receive some other form of punishment. The second school of thought is that a forgotten pencil should not keep a kid from learning. Your opinion on this topic will determine what course of action you are likely to take in your classroom. If you try to go against your natural instincts, you are more likely to fail at consistently enforcing the rule.

However you decide to handle missing materials, do not reduce academic grades because of lack of supplies. When you affect students' grades, you interfere with one of the main reasons why the students are in your class in the first place—learning. Other effective punishments can be devised to help teach responsibility.

23 Develop a Tardiness Plan

Methods of dealing with tardiness vary from school to school and teacher to teacher. The best systems are those that are school-wide and strictly enforced. For example, a school might have a "tardy card," which allows students to be late to a total of three classes per semester. When the student is late, the instructor signs the tardy card. If the student does not have her tardy card or it is full, then she gets a referral for tardiness. An additional component to this system really seems to motivate students: If they get through the semester without a single signature on their cards, the card gets entered in a drawing for prizes.

If your school does not have a unified policy or does not enforce the policy they do have, then it is up to you as the teacher to come up with a fair and consistent way of handling inevitable tardiness. If you ignore tardiness, it will increase and cause problems in your class. The ways to handle this issue are varied, and some methods are better and more appropriate than others. Some examples of methods used include locking students out of the room, giving detention for tardiness, giving on-time quizzes, and creating your own version of the tardy card for your class.

Institute a Late-Work Policy

You need to examine your beliefs about the purpose of education. If you believe that even though the work is done late it is important enough to be completed, then you need to allow for some sort of late work.

Since a late-work policy is a necessity, your job is to come up with an effective and enforceable plan. You need to try and find something that does not require a great deal of bookkeeping on your part. Your plan also needs to be quickly and consistently enforced.

One plan that seems to work well is to allow students one extra day to turn in late work and to penalize that work by a certain percentage. (For example, you might take ten or twenty points off the top.) However, for this to be effective you need to have a system for turning in this work. You might tell your students that late work must be turned in before the bell rings. If you have a pen handy as you stand by the door accepting the late work, you can immediately mark down the penalty on the paper. That way you will not forget how much each assignment needs to be reduced.

25 Make Students Make Up Work

Your policy for dealing with makeup work should be consistent with the school's policy on excused and unexcused absences. Most schools will issue a policy determining whether students are allowed to make up work. Some will even include a time frame for students to turn in their work. However, if your school does not give you this type of direction, then you need to come up with a policy of your own.

If students are making up work after an excused absence, it needs to be very clear to them what they need to do and when they need to turn in the work. An excellent way to accomplish this is to create an "Assignment Book." This is a notebook for each class in which you or a student you designate writes down what was covered during the day, including any homework. The absent student is then responsible for looking at the notebook the day he or she returns and writing down the assignments. If a handout is required, these should be available next to the notebook so the students have easy access to them.

Establish Rules for Restroom Visits 26

It is up to you as a teacher to decide exactly how you are to handle requests to use the bathroom. Restroom use can be a sticky issue.

On one hand, you do not want to keep a student who really has to go. On the other hand, this privilege is easily abused. The best policy is to allow students to use the restroom according to your set class rules. If you feel that a student is abusing this privilege then you have every right to discuss this with the administration and the student's parents. Usually, this problem can be solved through quick intervention.

A problem that arises with the decision to allow all students to use the restroom as needed is that it can quickly become disruptive. There is nothing worse than holding a discussion and having a student raise their hand only to discover they want to go to the bathroom. It is perfectly acceptable to require students to wait until you are at your desk or not addressing the entire class to ask to go to the restroom. You will want to create specific rules related to restroom use including the amount of time they are allowed to be gone and how many students you will allow out of your class at one time. Of course, if a student has a medical problem of which you have been informed, then you should allow that student to have a special restroom pass for emergencies.

27 Be the Boss

You must begin the year with an attitude of self-assurance. Always remember that you are the teacher, and that makes you the one in charge. Your attitude must be positive and full of high expectations. You should be friendly, but make it clear that you are ready to enforce your class rules.

If a teacher does not enforce the class rules strictly and consistently from day one, she will find it almost impossible to have her classroom under control. It is very difficult to become stricter, but this is the situation most new teachers get into during their first few years of teaching. New teachers usually proceed in the following manner:

1. They start off with the desire to have kids like them.
2. They lose control of their classroom environment.
3. They decide to tighten down on the rules.
4. They lose their sense of humor.
5. They lose their students' attention and respect.
6. Misbehavior increases.

A much better prospect is to start the year in a stern manner. That way, you can ease up as the year goes on. It is much easier to relax the rules later than it is to tighten the reins in class halfway through the year. When you do find that you can relax the rules a bit, students will enjoy the change while still realizing that if they do not follow the class rules, a working system is already in place to curb their misbehavior.

Plan to Discipline

A discipline plan is best when it is straightforward and easy to follow at a moment's notice. A good rule is the "three strikes" policy. This means that in most instances, the students will follow through three steps to get to the highest tier of the discipline plan. Here's a sample discipline plan with three steps:

1. Student's name gets written on board.
2. A checkmark goes next to student name.
3. Student sits in time-out.

This type of system needs to be adapted to the level of the students and to your particular needs. Other examples of disciplinary tactics that are often used include the following:

- Giving after-school detention
- Assigning sentences for student to write
- Requiring student to help clean the classroom
- Calling the parents
- Giving time-out
- Sending the child to the principal, guidance counselor, or the administrator designated for disciplinary action

Once you have decided on your particular discipline plan, you need to post it where all students can see it.

29 Enforce All Your Rules

You now have class rules and a posted discipline plan. However, that's not enough to have great classroom management. You need to follow through.

To be fair and consistent, you should follow the steps of the discipline plan for every student. With that said, there will be times when a student misbehaves so outrageously that you have no choice but to jump right to level three on the plan. For example, if you have a student who gets up in the middle of the class, cusses at you and the rest of the class, and then leaves, you would not simply follow the first step in the plan. You would go right ahead and write that student a referral. This is just common sense and good behavior management.

As you teach your lesson, make sure that you don't interrupt the flow to enforce discipline. Your discipline plan should not require you to stop everything to deal with minor misbehaviors. For example, if two students are passing notes to each other during a class discussion, do not interrupt your class to discuss this with them which could lead to a confrontation.

Instead, follow your discipline procedure. A good thing to practice is to continue to speak even as you move to complete a task. Keep talking as you write the students' names on the board. This shows students that you have a handle on things even as you are teaching them their lesson.

Listen Actively

An important part of classroom management involves your listening skills. Too many teachers do not actually listen to what their students are saying, and the kids quickly pick up on this. It is in your best interest to hone your listening skills. Just the simple act of listening can help calm an escalating situation.

Active listening is a learned skill that teaches you to fully listen and respond to others in the most effective manner possible. At first the practice of active listening might seem awkward. However, with practice it will become second nature to you.

To become an active listener, you need to give the speaker your full attention. Don't multitask while listening. When that person has finished speaking, you repeat in your own words what you heard. For example, if you heard, "I just can't do math," then you might respond with, "You are having a hard time understanding this assignment?" Then you give the speaker a chance to correct your interpretation. This achieves two goals: It cuts down on misunderstandings, and it makes the speaker feel that you are really listening.

31 Try a Little Humor!

It cannot be stressed enough that humor is your most effective tool as a teacher. Humor can defuse a quickly escalating situation. It reduces tension and allows your students to see that you are a real person. Do not think that to be humorous, you need to be a standup comedian. But if you can find the humor in a situation, don't be afraid to let this show. You will find that students will listen closer because they find your class more enjoyable.

One type of humor that teachers often use is sarcasm. You will discover that not all students will respond equally to sarcasm. It is important that you stay away from biting sarcasm, especially when dealing with younger children. Many younger students have not progressed to the point where they understand that sarcasm is not to be taken literally. Some older students can feel that sarcasm is threatening. You do not want your attempts at humor to be made at the expense of one of your students, which could lead to the alienation of that student in your class.

With that said, sarcasm, when used effectively, does have its place. Students are so used to hearing sarcasm on television that it seems normal to them. Just make sure that you really know a student before you joke around with them so they understand where you are coming from. If you do use sarcasm, try to direct it at situations and not people. The misuse of sarcasm can easily lead to the complaint that you really do not care about your students.

Be Specific When You Praise Students 32

Praise is a powerful tool that can really make a difference. Studies have shown that specific praise is very effective, while general praise is not. In other words, saying, "Johnny, excellent job adding those numbers," is much better than saying, "Great job, class." Keep this in mind when you praise or reward your students.

To make praise mean something, it must be given at the appropriate time. For example, if a student has a partially correct answer, you should not heap praise on him for answering the question correctly. Instead, you should point out the part of his answer that is correct and then help him dissect the question to come up with the complete answer.

Another point about praise is that it must be evenly administered. It is not a good idea or really fair to keep praising the same one or two students in the class. Your students will construe this as favoritism, and the frequently praised students may become objects of ridicule and resentment. Remember, even if you don't mean to play favorites, it is what the students perceive that matters.

33 Positively Reinforce the Right Way

Praise is one form of positive reinforcement for students that should be given immediately after a praiseworthy behavior has occurred. Rewards on the other hand are planned events for a series of good behaviors. For example, you might consider giving students a reward if a certain percentage of them pass an important test or for excellent participation in a classroom simulation. If you have behavioral problems in class, you might devise a reward system for encouraging good behavior. Rewards and praise create a positive reinforcement system for your class which is an important tool in your teaching arsenal.

It is important to remember when employing positive reinforcement the teachings of B. F. Skinner. Skinner's theory on operant conditioning showed that rewards are much more effective when they do not occur regularly. In other words, intermittent rewards mean more and have a greater effect than routine rewards. Students who never know when a reward might happen will behave better than those who know that you never give out rewards on Tuesdays.

Watch Out for Negative Reinforcement

34

One problem with the term negative reinforcement is that it is often confused with punishment. These are not the same thing. Negative reinforcement occurs when a painful behavior is stopped or avoided by redirection to a new behavior. Thus, punishment is always coupled with positive direction.

Let's say you have a student who has a problem with tardiness. She is punished every time she is tardy, and tardiness becomes a painful behavior for her. If that same student happens to come to class earlier one day, and she is met with a positive reaction from you, that's negative reinforcement. The more often she is early and experiences the positive reaction, the more likely she is to continue arriving early. It is not necessarily the punishment itself that caused the change but the punishment paired with the positive reaction for correct behavior.

When you mix positive and negative reinforcement techniques in your class, you will find that behavior modification becomes easier. Just punishing for misbehavior is not enough. Praising and rewarding correct behaviors makes this system extremely powerful.

35 Call the Parents When . . .

Contacting the student's parents is one of the most neglected aspects of successful teaching. The reason for this neglect is obvious and borne of necessity: Teachers often do not have the time to make the necessary phone calls to parents. However, if you want to ensure parental support and increase good behavior, find the time to make that phone call.

One method for making phone calls a little more manageable is to divide the total number of students you teach by the number of weeks in a grading period. For example, if you teach 150 students in a six-week grading period, then you would need to call twenty-five parents each week to reach them all.

Because this can be a lot of work in an already overloaded schedule, you might consider altering your call schedule by dividing your students into categories of need: high, medium, and low. High-need students are those who are having a very difficult time or who are having major behavioral problems in class. Medium-need students are those who are barely getting by. Low-need students are doing well in your course.

You should definitely contact the parents of all your high-need students and set goals for yourself with the other two groups. For example, you might try to reach half the parents of your medium-need students and maybe a quarter of the parents in the low-need group.

Get Results from Parent-Teacher Conferences

Nothing can replace sitting down one-on-one and talking to the parents of your students. A conference is a good opportunity to share with parents your methods for lessons and grading as well as the quality of work their child is turning in. However, parent-teacher conferences can be very stressful events. Some teachers find it difficult to be questioned by parents. Further, if the parents are not responsive to your observations, they can become confrontational.

To prevent a negative reaction, it is very important that you come to parent-teacher conferences prepared. It is helpful if you call and talk to the parent on the phone before the conference so you have a basis for mutual discussion once the conference starts. You should be honest about your concerns and observations, but you should also be tactful in your delivery. Remember, the parents you are meeting with love their children. If you have a bad report, it might pain them to hear it. Some parents will probably react with denial because it is easier than acceptance.

Another effective technique is to arrive at a parent-teacher conference with a plan in mind to help a struggling student. In other words, have some solutions in hand to give parents to try, and help them if they are unsure of what to do. It is important that you and the student's parents work toward the same goals because if you are clashing, the students will definitely pick that up and capitalize on it.

Part Three

Organizational Know-How

An unorganized teacher often has a hard time controlling student behavior. On the other hand, a teacher who has devoted some thought, time, and effort to room organization will find many housekeeping issues easier to handle. Good organization will help you cut down on disruptions while maximizing learning time. Organizing yourself and your room does not have to be a boring task, so start the year with a good and convenient organizational system in place.

37 Set Up and Seat Your Kids

One of the first decisions you will make is how to organize your room. You will most likely begin by placing your student's desks.

Traditionally, student desks are placed in rows. If you wish, you can try other methods of organization like placing them in a large circle or in small groups. Just be careful jumping into other sorts of desk arrangements because these can lead to more distractions for your students.

A good alternative is to have the desks arranged in rows, but have the students move them for special assignments.

Assigned Seats

It is in your best interest to assign seats for your students. This aids in learning names and in keeping students under control.

If you allow students to choose their own seats have them pick on the first day of class. Students will enjoy the freedom to choose their seats in the beginning. However, realize that students will sit next to their friends, which can lead to behavior problems. Poor-performing students may choose to sit in the back of the room.

On the other hand, if you prepare a seating chart before the students arrive, this might cause some initial grumbling. You should make it clear to your students from the beginning that you will be making adjustments to the seating chart after the first two weeks and then again once each grading period.

Decide about Your Desk

Where your desk is placed will greatly depend on the location of the chalkboard and student desks. There are numerous ways you can place your desk. Most teachers choose to place their desk in the front of the room with the students facing the desk. It might be to one side of the chalkboard. This allows you quick access to the board and will allow you to look at your students as they work quietly at their desks.

However, you are not required to place your desk at the front. In fact, many teachers find that placing their desks behind the students can be very effective. For one thing, if you allow students to choose their seats, usually those who need the most help or are the most disruptive will sit in the back. They will do this even if your desk happens to be located there. This can lead to better classroom control.

Another benefit of sitting behind the students is that you do not cause as great a disruption for them as they work. If you are shuffling papers or working on the computer, they will not be distracted by your actions. You will also have some privacy to complete additional tasks other than teaching that you have each day.

39 Take Time to Decorate

Once you have all of your big items placed, you can decorate your room. Most teachers have to pay for their own decorations. However, some schools do give teachers a small discretionary budget. At the very least, you will want to have some construction paper and a cardboard border to go around your bulletin boards along with a few posters or visuals that are connected to your curriculum.

You will want to think carefully about possible distractions as you place posters and create billboards. There is a fine line between an interesting and well-decorated room and one that is so cluttered students will have problems concentrating. If you find your students spend more time looking at your posters than working, you might want to consider removing some of them from the walls.

As the year goes on, you will want to replace posters and billboards to either enhance your lessons or to highlight quality student work. This is especially true with younger students where you can highlight their creativity and decorate your room at the same time. Even older children will enjoy seeing their work posted so don't be afraid to put their work up around the room.

Stock Up on These Important Supplies

40

As you gather together your classroom supplies, you will definitely want to have the following:

- Chalk and/or markers
- Erasers
- Pens, pencils, and paper
- Pencil sharpener
- Stapler and scissors
- Thumbtacks and paperclips
- Tape and glue
- File folders

If you can get these items through administration or other teachers, then you have a good basis for what you will need. Of course, you need to adapt this list to your situation.

You will find that you will be better organized if you divide your room into separate areas. For example, you might have a location where all of your art supplies go. You could have containers holding rulers, glue sticks, markers and colored pencils, and construction paper. This will enable students to return materials to their proper place when they are finished.

Think about the different tasks you plan to do in your classroom before deciding on a final location for your supplies. Make a list of the top four to six tasks you and/or your students would complete that require supplies. Then assign each task a location in your room. The supplies associated with each of the tasks should be located in these separate areas.

41 Take Textbook Distribution into Account

It is important that you keep accurate records when you assign textbooks to each student so that the students are held responsible for missing and lost texts. You must have a clear, easy-to-use method for assigning texts as part of your professional responsibilities. Most schools have their teachers follow the same system, typically having students fill out textbook cards. You should store these cards in a safe place and always keep extras handy. You should also keep track of books during the year by holding periodic textbook checks.

Class Sets

Some schools do not have enough texts to provide each student with their own copy to take home.

Class sets can be a nightmare if you do not have a good system in place. Students have a tendency to walk out of the classroom with their books. Your system for handling this situation should be easy to use and understand.

One method is to assign a book to each desk. It's not difficult to visually check at the end of each class to make sure all the books are there. Another method is to assign each student a book for in-class use. Students would be responsible for getting their book before the period starts and then replacing them when the class was finished.

Offer Other Reading Material

Many teachers have other books in their classrooms that they allow students to borrow and read. This is especially the case in language arts classes, where students are required to read other books for assignments. If you plan on having books that students can borrow, you need to create a checkout system.

Once again, make sure to create a system that is easy to understand and use. You should definitely restrict book checkouts to specific times in your class. That way, you will not have students disrupting lessons by trying to check out books. Make sure that students clearly understand the procedures for checking out books in your class.

Keep a checkout sheet at your desk. You can choose to have the students be responsible for writing down the book's title, their name, the date, and the class they are in while you watch, or you can take care of writing it yourself. This provides you with a record of who has borrowed your books so you'll know whom to contact if they are not returned.

Make sure that students understand your policy concerning book checkouts. For example, you might only allow a book to be checked out for two weeks. This allows other students to have access to popular books.

43 Make a Plan for Your Paperwork

As a teacher, you'll find that you have to deal with a lot of paperwork. To stay organized, it's a good idea to set up a filing system. Give some thought to your filing system before you actually begin filing. A good exercise is to write down all of the major file headings that you think you will need. Try to make them intuitive. You will not want to spend a great deal of time going through your files to find a specific paper because you cannot remember the file headings you used.

A great system to try is color-coding. Pick a file color for each of the major categories of files. For example, you might have different colors for the following:

- School paperwork
- Student work
- Lesson plans
- Curriculum-specific information
- Professional development

Once you pick the categories, you can create files using the color-coded category system and place them together in your file cabinets. If you see a file lying on your desk, you will know without looking at it what category of file it is. If you would like to learn more about organizing your file system or your room itself, refer to *Organizing from the Inside Out,* by Julie Morgenstern. This book provides excellent systems to help you get your classroom organized.

44 Organize with These Tricks of the Trade

There are many other tools that teachers rely on to help create a more organized environment. Following are two ideas that you might find useful. However, don't forget that you can also ask your fellow teachers for systems that work for them.

Student Cards

All you need are some 3" x 5" cards and a container. Give each student a card, and tell them all to fill out the information you wish to know. You can write the exact format on the board so that all the cards will be filled out in the same manner. Here's the kind of information you may wish to ask:

- Name
- Address
- Phone number
- Date of birth
- Class period
- Parent name
- Parent's work/cell number

Student Calendars

It is very easy to create a blank calendar, print it out, and then give one to each student. You should write an agenda on the board each day, and then require the students to copy that agenda along with any homework you might assign onto their calendar. Then, you can periodically collect and check the calendars for completion.

45 Lean on Lesson Plans

A good lesson plan is one that sees the "big picture" but includes detailed information for each activity. It's a good idea to organize your lesson plans as a unit plan. Each unit plan will cover a particular topic, and may be broken down into daily plans. An effective unit plan will include the following:

Objective(s): While easy to ignore, identifying objectives from the beginning will vastly simplify instruction and assessment.

Activities: The meat of your lesson plan will be the various activities you use to teach students what you want them to know.

Time estimates: Including a time estimate for each activity allows you to divide your unit plan into days and periods of time.

Required materials: Spend some time writing down exactly what materials you need for each activity so that you will be better prepared for your lesson.

Alternatives: It is always wise to plan ahead for absent students, especially if a large part of your plan is a simulation that can be hard to make up.

Assessments: Deciding in the beginning how you are going to assess your students will help focus your instruction on what the students actually need to learn.

Establish an Objective

When a teacher takes the time to determine what he wants his students to learn from a lesson, he is creating a learning objective. These objectives help shape the curriculum and daily lessons of the course. Often, the learning objectives for a course are mandated by your district or state. The federal government often publishes guidelines, which some schools ask their teachers to follow. Further, outside forces like high-stakes testing can affect the learning objectives of classroom teachers. Overall, it is important for you as a teacher to combine these elements and add your own personal vision to create an effective learning environment.

Take some time as you create your lessons to truly decide what you want your students to learn from the material. An effective exercise is to decide the top three to five points you want students to take away from a lesson. Make sure you stress these important points while teaching the material. Write the points you wish to stress on the board or on a handout to help students frame any notes they take.

Make sure that any assessments you create also include these important points. Students will learn what you stress. Conversely, if you spend an inordinate part of your lesson on something that you feel is not that important to learn, you are wasting precious educational time.

47 Mark Your Calendar!

The first step you should take as you start lesson planning is to sit down and create a school calendar. Once you have your blank calendar in front of you, mark off all the vacation days. Then, mark off any dates for testing (if you know what they are at this point). If you know an event is going to happen in a month but you are not sure of the date, make a note at the top of that month's calendar page.

When you are done, count the number of days that are left. This is the maximum number of days you think that you will have to actually teach your students. Now, subtract one more day each month to account for unexpected events, and you will have a fairly accurate count of what you can expect each month.

Once you have this determined, you can start deciding your units of study and how many days you will need for each unit. To determine this, you will need to work closely with your texts and other resources to see how much material you have available. With this tentative time frame worked out, pencil in the starting date for each unit on the calendar.

This calendar will be the foundation for your curriculum. It gives you an overall picture of what you are going to be covering when. The calendar allows you to determine if you are on track. You can then adjust lessons to make sure that you meet your curriculum objectives.

Work with State and National Standards 48

Each state has its own system for developing standards, and methods vary from district to district. While there are some national curriculum standards developed by different councils and groups, there are no "official" national standards that all teachers and schools must follow. Today, there are arguments both for and against the creation of national standards for all teachers to follow.

By allowing states to define their own standards and not mandating national standards, the federal government lets states determine what is important to them. The argument is that if the national government created standards, this type of individual focus would be impossible to maintain.

On the flip side, if national standards were mandated, proponents claim that curriculum would be standardized across the nation. It would become much more likely that the information learned in American history class would not vary from state to state. This issue of state versus national standards will continue to be debated for quite some time.

In any event, it is your job as a teacher to keep apprised of the state and possible national standards that should be followed for each course you teach. You might want to investigate through your state Department of Education ways that you can get involved. Many states create committees including classroom teachers that periodically help rewrite standards for each subject.

49 Learn to Handle High-Stakes Testing

Teachers across the nation are increasingly faced with the need to prepare their students for high-stakes testing. For example, at this time all students in Florida must pass the Florida Comprehensive Assessment Test (FCAT) in order to graduate from high school. Further, funding and school grades are based in part on the results of this test.

The goal of tests such as the FCAT is to ensure that students meet minimum levels of achievement at different grades throughout their school careers. The tests are also built with a desire to create educational accountability. In a perfect world, teachers would not have to change what they were teaching in order to fully prepare students for tests like the FCAT. They would test the curriculum that teachers are supposed to teach. However, many times these tests do not mirror the curriculum taught in the classroom. Therefore, teachers spend time preparing the students for the test in addition to covering the curriculum for their courses. If this is the case in your state, then you will need to account for this as you make your overall calendar and your individual unit plans.

50 Capture the Ideas that Are All Around You

You should not rely solely on the teacher's edition of your textbook to create your lesson plans. Even though they have some excellent resources and ideas, exclusively relying on them could cause you to miss out on some great educational experiences for your students.

Online Resources

The Internet is an excellent source of free material for lesson plans. However, it is important to be discerning about the quality of the lessons you find online.

Other Teachers

Rely on other teachers to give you a sense of what does and does not work. Other educators might have effective lessons that you can use or adapt.

Students as a Resource

Sometimes students will bring up issues that could form the basis of great lessons. Usually, when students are interested enough in a topic to ask questions about it, they will be engaged in lessons covering that topic.

The World Around You

Using real-world examples will help students connect to your curriculum. Sources for educational ideas are all around us. Remain aware of the latest trends and ideas, and try to find ways to incorporate them.

51 Find Time for the Most Important Things

It's tough to know how much to include in a new lesson. While you can gain some insight into timing through years of experience, even veteran teachers occasionally overplan or underprepare. If you have to choose, err on the side of overplanning. It is much easier to cut things out of a plan or continue it on the next day than to fill up twenty minutes. With this said, your goal should be to always plan for about ten minutes longer than you think you will need. Keep a stock of "mini-lessons" that you can pull out as needed in order to fill up any extra time you might have.

Effective Use of Cliffhangers

One technique that effective teachers employ is to use cliffhangers at the end of a day's lesson. When you are excited about your subject, your students will be as well. Leave the kids little hints to entice them for the next day's lesson. This excitement will carry over to the next day.

Cliffhangers can take many forms, including handouts, questions on the board, or brief discussions that leave questions unanswered until the next day. Keep the cliffhangers in mind as you create your lessons.

Make Homework Count 52

Part of lesson planning is designing your homework assignments. To avoid creating ineffective assignments, you need to begin by defining your beliefs about the purpose of homework. Homework should not simply be a way of burdening students with busy work. Assignments should reinforce central ideas and provide students with methods for exhibiting knowledge in unique ways. Whenever possible, make homework connect to real life. Give students the opportunity to practice using the information that you have taught them, so that they can learn to make connections between what they learn and current events or skills that they will use throughout their lives.

A further consideration you need to give when creating homework assignments is how much time and effort you wish to put into grading student work. Remember, you will need to grade all the homework you assign. This does not mean that you should avoid important assignments like essays or laboratory reports. However, it does mean that you might think about placing easier-to-grade (not necessarily easier-to-complete) assignments in between those that are more time-consuming.

53 Let Your Kids Have a Life Outside School

So how much homework should you give? You should strive to have enough to reinforce and teach the core ideas, but not so much that students have time for little more than homework. This is a fine line to walk.

If you are an elementary school teacher, you know exactly what homework your students have because you are in charge of assigning all work. You can control exactly how long students are to work each evening. You decide what you feel your students need and assign accordingly.

Middle school teachers often work on teams and can join together to control the amount of homework students are assigned. The real problem lies with high school teachers who do not work in coherent teams and therefore cannot consult with other teachers to control homework for each student. Generally, this does not cause major issues in average classes. However, when students are participating in honors and advanced placement courses, they can run into a real problem with exorbitant amounts of homework.

If students have to work five or more hours every evening to complete their assignments, then they probably are not getting enough exercise or sleep to be healthy. This is something to keep in mind.

54 Plan for Lesson Flexibility

Change and interruptions will occur more often than you will care to remember as you teach. Therefore, it is important that you keep a flexible attitude as you approach your lesson plans. With that said, there will be times when you will need to complete important assignments without interruption. This might happen with certain science experiments and timed tests. Therefore, these assignments must be given on days where you have the least chance of interruption. You can let those teachers with classrooms near you along with your administrator know when you have such an assignment. This might help cut down on interruptions. In other words, investigate and try not to assign a time-imperative assignment on a day when a planned fire alarm or other planned interruption is scheduled to occur.

Be aware that despite all the planning, you will eventually have to face the inevitable and scrap a great lesson because the time was stolen by an unexpected event. In the end, it is important to have a flexible attitude at all times, if for nothing more than your own health.

Part Four

Make the Most of Your Teaching Time

Instructional time is precious. While some days it might seem like the year will never end, if you do the math you will figure that your time with students in class is very limited. The attention span of students is such that even long stretches of time are broken up by disruptions, which reduce your effective teaching time. Therefore, it is important to use every minute you have to help students get the best educational experience possible.

55 Engage Your Students

When you are teaching, your goal should be to have students engaged from the moment they walk in your classroom to the moment they leave. While this is never fully possible with every student, it is a worthy goal that will lead to positive choices for you and your students. One way to begin each class on the right foot is to have a warm-up or "bell ringer" waiting for them as they walk through the door.

Warm-ups are very short assignments that students complete within the first few minutes of class while you are completing important housekeeping tasks like taking attendance. Warm-ups make it clear to students that you mean for them to work when they are in your class.

Warm-ups also have the benefit of giving focus to the lesson for the day or even providing a review of the previous day's lesson. Students are often asked simple questions based on information learned. You can ask them for short, thoughtful responses to questions that require them to integrate their learning into the real world.

It is imperative that if you choose to use warm-ups, you do so consistently. They should be done the same way each day, so there is no confusion. Consider having the warm-up on the board or overhead and waiting for the students as they come in.

Write in Journals Every Day

Some teachers find that journal writing is a good way to keep students occupied until class begins. Students are asked to keep a notebook, which they either leave in class or take with them and turn in each week. Students write during the first five minutes of class. The teacher can assign a topic for the day, allow students to write what they want, or combine the two methods. Many times teachers will guide their students' journals to follow the curriculum of the course but then allow them a day of freedom every once in a while where they can just share their thoughts.

The advantage to journal writing is that students get a chance to express themselves. This allows you the chance to get to know your students a little better through their journals. Some students feel safer asking for help on paper than in front of the class and journal writing provides them this opportunity.

However, journals do pose some problems for teachers. For one thing, they have to be graded. Grading journals can take some time. Also, because of the freedom inherent in journal writing, students can sometimes discuss topics that are inappropriate. It is your job to make sure that students know your expectations about their journal. Just because you are allowing students to share their thoughts and opinions does not mean they have the right to write whatever they want.

57 Stay on Top of Attendance

Probably the most important housekeeping task you will have to complete each day is taking attendance. This is important not only for record-keeping purposes but, more importantly, for legal issues. If a student is reported as absent in your class, and they do something illegal, you will have no further issue in the matter. However, if you mark a student as present in your class when they were actually absent or, worse yet, if you have no idea if a student was present or absent on a particular day, you can encounter difficulties from both the administration and the authorities if illegal or dangerous activities occur.

Another consideration is the importance of having accurate records in times of emergencies like tornadoes or fires. Most schools require teachers to take their attendance books when they have to leave their classroom for a fire alarm to help ensure an accurate count is made.

While important, attendance records can be time-consuming to keep. In the beginning of the year, taking attendance out loud can help you reinforce the name learning process. However, you should strive to take attendance quietly after you have learned the students' names. Make sure to use the school-wide system for marking unexcused and excused absences along with tardies.

Collect Homework the Right Way

58

Collecting homework is another necessary task that should be done efficiently so that it will not take up a lot of class time. If you are teaching in a situation where students are moving from class to class as in secondary school, then you might decide to collect homework as students walk into your room each period. If you consistently enforce this rule, then students will learn that they are to have their homework ready before they walk in your class. This eliminates the time necessary to complete this task.

An alternative is to have a "homework box" that is only available to students before the bell rings and class begins. Students must turn in their homework before the time you designate, or it is considered late. This system is difficult to keep fair because a student might be late but have a valid excuse. Therefore, you might consider allowing the first three minutes after the bell rings as additional turn-in time.

It is not a good idea to accept homework at the end of a period. Students will quickly catch on to your habit and will finish their homework during class time. In fact, if you give homework too early in a period, some students will probably stop listening and begin working on it. Therefore, it is best to collect homework at the very beginning of the period and assign homework at the very end.

59 Repeat and Review Your Key Points

Most teachers spend a few moments reviewing the previous day's lesson before heading off into new territory. This helps students make connections from day to day and shows them the framework for learning and building on previous knowledge. Warm-ups can help begin this review. After students complete their warm-up, and you have completed your necessary housekeeping tasks, you can move right into review.

You only need to spend a few minutes going over the key points in review. At this time, it is best if you question your students and allow them to show you their knowledge. That can help you clear up any errors they might have in their thinking and allow you to judge the effectiveness of the previous day's lesson. This review should easily transition into the lesson for the day.

At the End of the Period

After you have taught a lesson, spend a few minutes going over the key points. This can help you see if students understand what you have taught before they complete any assigned readings or homework on the same topic.

End-of-the-period review is most effective when you have completed an alternative learning activity, like a role-play or simulation. By bringing students back to the reality of the classroom through review, you can reinforce the key points they should have learned.

Organize and Discipline

Organization can seem difficult at first because it requires some discipline on your part. However, if you are not organized, you will waste time looking for items or determining what's next in your lesson. For example, if you do not have the quizzes where you can easily get them for Step 3, then your students will probably get off task as you look for them.

You should have students learn that at the end of assignments and tests they complete in class, they are always to pass their papers to the front so you can collect them. If you spend time walking around the class taking papers, you and your students will lose momentum. Think in terms of efficiency for yourself and your students.

One final idea that can help make this transition easier, especially if you plan to have a lot of small-group activities, is to have students practice at the beginning of the year moving their chairs into position. During the first week of school you can have students do desk-moving drills. Your goal is to have a quiet and quick transition in order to keep talking and distractions down to a minimum.

61 Take Control of Your Time

If you lose control of your class as you deal with disruptions, you will find that it takes a long time for students to get back on task. Therefore, it is important to keep disruptions to a minimum.

For minor disruptions, it might be enough to call on students to answer questions or hand them small notes that say "See me after class." Writing students' names on the board can be effective for younger students. However, realize that some students might try to argue with you when you do this. Do not engage in this type of verbal sparring in front of the rest of your class. Instead, tell the student to discuss it with you after class.

What should you do with the overzealous students who will cause disruptions for you by being so involved that they dominate your class? It is important that you rein these students in, not only for your own sanity but also for the student. These students can often be the target of other students who consider them "know-it-alls" or "goody two-shoes." You might want to have a discreet discussion with this type of student, explaining that you are impressed with their learning and their attitude but also explaining what you are trying to do in the classroom. Make them a part of your team for creating an effective learning environment for all students.

Be Ready for Downtime

62

Despite overplanning and the use of reviews, you will sometimes be faced with an extra five to ten minutes at the end of class. What do you do with this time? Some teachers allow students to simply work on their homework or even chat with their friends. However, with the belief that time is precious, you might want to consider creating some mini-lessons to fill up this time.

Short lessons do not necessarily have to relate to the topic you are currently teaching. You might have a newspaper with you each day in case downtime arises, and you can discuss topics in the news. Newspapers can be effective for all classes. For example, math teachers can discuss the use and abuse of statistics, science teachers can start discussions based on the technology section of newspapers, and English teachers can have students analyze grammar.

Another idea is to invest in some puzzle books. It is fun to pull out "lateral-thinking puzzles" and have students work together to come up with the answer. Similarly, you might pull out trivia questions and have students compete in teams. You could keep a running tab of which team is in the lead throughout the year.

The leftover minutes in a period are a great time to get students to really think. They can also build interest in your class. Students are allowed to have a little more fun than usual. Think before you allow these moments to be wasted by letting students talk amongst themselves.

63 Get to Know the Three Learning Types

There are three major approaches that students take to learning: visual, auditory, and tactile/kinesthetic. These are called learning styles. Each person has a particular learning style that is best for their intake and comprehension of new information. Visual learners generally think in terms of pictures and learn best from visuals and handouts. Auditory learners learn best by listening. They usually like lecture and classroom discussions, and they might need to read written material aloud in order to fully understand it. Tactile/kinesthetic learners learn through touching, feeling, and experiencing the world around them. They do well with hands-on experiments, but they may have a hard time sitting through lectures and notes.

Many people have a single learning style that they do best with. However, unless someone is physically disabled, they can actually learn through all three learning styles. Therefore, do not think that just because a student is a kinesthetic learner (which many of your students will be) that you always have to have hands-on experiments and simulations. What's important is that you understand that there are different approaches to learning and the way you learn best may not be the way that your students learn best.

Cater to Your Kids' Styles 64

As a teacher, you will find that many of your students are best at tactile/kinesthetic learning. Because traditional classroom teaching techniques often target visual and auditory learning styles, these students get bored and have trouble concentrating.

You should try to incorporate all three learning styles into your lessons. It is not hard to combine visual and auditory learning because you can provide students with visuals and graphics as you give them notes. However, it can be hard to incorporate tactile/kinesthetic learning all of the time. Don't try to force the issue, but whenever possible, look for lessons that lend themselves to this type of learning. For example, simulations and role-playing allows students to get more hands-on and actually experience what they are learning.

Ineffective Use of Learning Styles

As you consider your students' dominant learning styles, don't go overboard and assume that they cannot learn in other ways. While it might be more difficult for them, they should still learn to adapt to all types of instruction. You can help them prepare for less sympathetic teachers by showing them techniques they can use to enhance their learning through each type of style.

65 9 Measures of Intelligence Revealed

The theory of multiple intelligences, as devised by Howard Gardner, proposes that the traditional intelligence quotient (IQ) measure of intelligence does not illuminate the whole or even a significant part of the overall picture. According to Gardner, there are nine multiple intelligences, and each person has their own strengths and weaknesses:

1. Linguistic intelligence
2. Logical-mathematical intelligence
3. Spatial intelligence
4. Bodily kinesthetic intelligence
5. Musical intelligence
6. Interpersonal intelligence
7. Intrapersonal intelligence
8. Naturalist intelligence
9. Existential Intelligence

Teachers tend to focus their instruction on the first two types of intelligence: linguistic and logical-mathematical. However, many students are not strong in both or even one of these areas. You need to keep this in mind.

Adjusting lesson plans does not mean that you need to meet all of the multiple intelligences in all lessons. What it does mean is that you should provide some variety in your instruction. For example, in a social studies class studying the 1960s, you could play protest music for discussion to meet the musical intelligence.

Vary Your Skills for Better Overall Instruction

66

The information presented so far should lead you to the conclusion that varied instruction is not only desirable—it is a necessity. Varying instruction means that you do not just rely on lecture or discussions or even cooperative learning. In fact, teachers who rely too much on role-playing and cooperative learning are committing just as great of an error as those who focus on lecture. It also means that you do not teach to just one learning style or hit upon only one or two of the multiple intelligences.

Varying instruction is also important because it helps build interest in your class. Even if you have a student who works best when given an assignment to read from a book and answer questions, they will enjoy and benefit from other forms of learning.

As teachers, we often need to consider that we are not stuck in the lower levels of Bloom's taxonomy. In other words, while it is important to teach kids to recall information like multiplication tables, it is equally if not more important to teach them to analyze and synthesize information. Critical thinking skills can be used in all methods of delivering instruction.

67 Lecture—Only Sometimes

While you should not lecture to your students every day, there is a time and a place for a lecture. Lectures will often provide students with the greatest amount of material in the shortest amount of time. However, you need to ensure that students know how to take notes before relying too much on lecture.

Note-taking can be a difficult task for many students. You can help them immediately by giving them some shorthand abbreviations for terms you often use. However, this is not enough to help students succeed. Many students have problems understanding how to take notes because they cannot discern what is important. Therefore, when you are first teaching your students how to listen to lectures, it is important to teach them verbal cues that teachers use to inform students that an important point has been made.

One example of a verbal clue is repetition. If you repeat an important point two or three times, students should realize that this is something they need to write down and remember. Similarly, if you write words and points down on the board or overhead as you are talking, students will realize that they too need to be jotting down the information. You can be even more overt and make a statement before each really important piece of information that lets the students know they need to remember what you are about to say.

Have Discussions in Groups—with Rules

An alternative to lecture is class discussion. The teacher will still present new material and the students will be required to answer questions and provide examples. In this way, students are much more involved in the learning process. However, unless you require participation, it can be hard to get everyone involved.

An alternative to whole group discussion is to break up the class into smaller groups of four to six students. Each group then receives a topic of discussion and questions they need to answer. The teacher is much further removed from this type of discussion, which can have both positive and negative side effects. As long as each group remains on task, holding small groups of discussion can be very rewarding.

Rules for Discussion

It is important that you set up some ground rules for your students during group discussions. Ensure that only one person is talking at a time. Make it clear that no one may make fun of another for their opinions. In a healthy discussion, it's normal for people to disagree, and your students need to learn how to respect the opinions of their peers.

It is your job to act as the facilitator and keep the discussion on topic. You may be faced with a student who has a different agenda and tries to move the discussion to irrelevant topics. Unless what the student brings up is something that needs to be discussed or is a teachable moment, you should not deviate from your original lesson plan.

69 Try Cooperative Learning Lessons

Cooperative learning is the practice of placing students into groups and having them work together to complete assignments. Much has been said and taught about the pros and cons of cooperative learning. Some educational professionals believe that teachers should predominantly use cooperative learning in their classes. However, a more balanced approach is needed to fully realize the power of cooperative learning.

Effective cooperative learning takes a lot of time on the teacher's part. It is quite easy to get students into groups and have them complete a worksheet together. However, this is not true cooperative learning. Instead, students should be given roles to fulfill in their group. The information presented must be interesting and challenging at the same time.

Overuse of cooperative learning can lead to boredom and issues between students. Most people have experienced working in a group where one or more members refuse to do anything. Unfortunately, in cooperative learning many teachers have a difficult time differentiating between students within a group. Instead, they just give the entire group the same grade regardless of whether only one person did the work or all of the students contributed to it. On the other hand, if teachers do try to differentiate between students, this can lead to hard feelings and further problems.

Teaching Them How to Learn Together

So how do you effectively use cooperative learning? As previously stated, you should give each student a role to fulfill in the group. Each role should have some part of the project that is their contribution. This will help them understand what they should be doing and it helps you divvy out the grades at the end of the lesson.

You should also provide students with a means for presenting their feelings on the effort put forth by each team member. You might pass out a form that asks each student to rate their own and their team members' work; each student should complete this form privately. If numerous members of a team agree that someone did not participate in the group, this can be combined with your own observations to determine grades.

It is also important to keep cooperative learning groups on task. Divide your cooperative learning lesson into chunks and tell your students when they should be moving to the next part of the lesson. Also, make sure to circulate through the room and directly observe what each group is doing.

71 Using Unique Lessons

Role-playing and debates can be highly effective forms of teaching. When students participate in these types of activities, they are fully engaged. In role-playing, students pretend to be other people and interact as these new persons. In debates, students argue two or more sides of an issue by bringing up facts and important points. If used correctly, these methods can create educational memories that will last a lifetime.

Role-playing and debates can get out of hand if you as a teacher do not have a handle on things. You need to have strict rules for each of the activities, and you must enforce them fairly and consistently. When students begin talking at the same time or making fun of each other, you need to stop them immediately.

Student participation is central to these types of activities, so you need to have rewards and penalties based on levels of participation. If you do not implement such a system, students will see less of a reason to become involved in the future.

Include All Students in the Lesson

72

It can be challenging to have all students participate in some activities. For example, having a debate with fifteen students on a side is unmanageable. A great technique for debates is to create teams of four or five students each and then have the rest of the class be the audience. Because the debating team has to do a lot of research and work before and during the debate, you need to make sure that the audience does a comparable amount of work.

Therefore, you should require audience members to also do some research before the debate begins and come up with questions that they wish to ask the debating teams at the conclusion of the debate. You could have them take notes during the debate. Finally, you could have these students "judge" which side won the debate.

Role-playing requires a lot of preparation on the part of the teacher before the activity even begins. You must have a clear purpose and understanding of what you wish to accomplish through this technique. You also need to give students enough time before the class to complete any research that you require of them.

When a role-playing lesson is finished, students need to be debriefed. To do this, you could have them create a reflection journal or answer questions stressing the information you feel was most important. Sometimes, students will really enjoy role-playing and even debating, but they will not necessarily understand what information they need to remember for future exams.

Part Five

Dealing with the Unexpected

Sometimes teaching can be a very difficult profession because there are aspects that are at the limits of your control. While you can maintain a level of discipline in your classroom through consistency and fairness, you still cannot control the uncontrollable. Prejudice and controversy will probably arise, especially in upper-level classes. School violence is a serious issue that cannot be ignored. Dealing with these and other uncertainties is one of the challenges of an effective educator.

73 Combat Prejudice in the Classroom

Any form of prejudice harms the learning environment. Stereotypes and put-downs should be prohibited in your class. The first clue that students have to your staunch attitude against prejudice should be your initial reaction to any stereotypical or prejudicial statements that are voiced. For example, if a student says something derogatory about a certain group of people, your reaction should be firm, swift, and forceful. With a serious expression, stare at the student in question and say something like, "That type of speech is not allowed in this classroom."

You need to be quick to stop offensive speech. If it gets out of hand, there will be hurt feelings and your classroom could become a battleground. This, of course, is to be avoided at all cost. Your classroom should be a safe haven for all students who feel that you welcome them despite their gender, religion, or ethnic background.

Freedom of Speech

Older students might argue with you concerning their right to voice their opinions. Students often bring up the Constitution and its protections for free speech. Point out to them that they do have the protection of the Constitution. However, according to the law, school is a special place. The Supreme Court has said that speech is not allowed that "materially and substantially" disrupts class. Any inflammatory speech against a group should be considered disruptive to the learning environment.

Stash Bad Thoughts Away

School is supposed to be a safe place. This concept includes physical safety, but it also means safety from hate and prejudice. It is the teacher's job to create this environment in the classroom.

There are many ways that you can create a prejudice-free atmosphere in your classroom. For one thing, you should be very welcoming to all students on the first day of class. You can also discuss the issue before it arises, announcing to your class that your room is a "prejudice-free zone." To make this more concrete and humorous for students, one of the most effective tools you can create is "The Box."

The Box is located in an imaginary space located right outside your door. Its purpose is to hold all the prejudices, stereotypes, and hatreds the students might have while they are in your class. As students come into your room, they are to leave these ideas, opinions, and words outside in The Box. Ultimately, you hope that by using this tool, you can help students leave their prejudices behind even when they leave your classroom.

75 Deal with the Controversy

Controversial topics will probably arise in most upper-level and some lower-level classes. Some topics will be inappropriate, and you will want to stop those discussions as soon as they begin. However, there will be times when you will want to address important topics that are timely. For example, if cloning is in the news, it might be a good time to discuss it in a government or science class. Your job as the teacher is to facilitate and lead the discussion in an appropriate manner.

One of the major items that you must be prepared to address is the way students frame their thoughts when talking about controversial topics. For example, it would not be appropriate at any time during a whole class discussion for students to begin teasing or name-calling others for their beliefs. Similarly, it would not be appropriate to allow students to speak in a stereotypical manner about others. It is best to require your students to prove any claims they make. In other words, if they are going to make an inflammatory statement, they better have the scientific proof to back it up.

76 Teach and Learn by Debate

Debates are an extremely important and effective tool for teaching students how to research and approach a topic. You should not shy away from them simply because they can lead to controversial discussions. You can minimize the problems associated with debates by following some simple steps:

1. Give students ample time to research their topics.
2. Make sure students know that inappropriate comments and speech will not be allowed.
3. Give all students a rubric explaining exactly how the debate will be graded.
4. Explain on your rubric that points will be deducted for stereotypical speech and name-calling.
5. Make it clear that all points introduced in the debate must be backed up by credible sources and require students to turn in a bibliography at the end.
6. Strictly limit speaking time, and make sure that only one student gets to speak at any time.
7. Allow for guided, open discussion at the end of a debate to talk about any important issues that might have come up during the debate.

Debating can be a lot of fun and is very interesting for both the students and the teacher. But don't let the fun distract you—it is still up to you to keep the students focused on the topic and speaking in an appropriate manner.

77 Recognize How Religion Fits

Religion is a very sticky subject because so many differing emotions and beliefs are involved. It would be good to remember that many of the world's wars began and were fought because of religion. Therefore, it is a good general rule for public school teachers to avoid the topic.

There are times, however, that you will be required by standards to teach about the world religions. The important thing to remember is to present the world religions in an even manner, not stereotyping any of them. Of course, the rules for dealing with religion differ depending on whether you teach in a public or a private school.

Public Schools

Because public schools are part of the government, public school teachers must faithfully follow the Constitution. This means that they may not "establish a . . . religion" through their classroom. In practice, this means that as a teacher, you must not impose your views and beliefs on your students. Federal courts have ruled that you may not even read a Bible silently during class, as this might sway a child's opinion about religion (*Helland v. South Bend Community School Corp*).

What should you do if a student asks you a question about your religious beliefs? In general, your school district will probably advise you to refrain from discussing specific religious viewpoints in a classroom setting. But you can state your religious preference.

78 Find a Place for Politics Too

Another topic that deserves special consideration is politics. While not as controversial as religion, politics can still cause teachers problems if not handled correctly. It is perfectly acceptable to share with your students your political party affiliation. However, it is not acceptable to stereotype or make fun of people whose beliefs are different than yours. Remember, many of these students' parents and families will have opinions that are diametrically opposed to your own.

It is best to avoid politics completely, if possible. However, this is not always feasible. Sometimes current events thrust politics into the spotlight. Also, you may be teaching a class like American Government, which requires you to address political issues. In that case, be very careful that these issues are approached in a neutral manner.

When dealing with students and their beliefs, use the Socratic method. Here's how this method works: You ask your students questions to try and get them to more precisely define exactly what they do believe and why they believe it. This does not mean that you cannot guide discussions, but it does mean that you should try to avoid imposing your views on your students.

79 Guard Against School Violence

One of the main things you can do to help prevent violent crimes at school is to watch for warning signs from your students. Some examples of warning signs include:

- A sudden change in interest level at school
- An obsession with violence
- Sudden change in attitude or mood swings
- Clues from writing, signs of isolation and despair
- Sudden violent and angry outbursts
- Talking about dying or death
- Talking about bringing weapons to school
- Indications of violence toward animals

If you see these signs in one or more students, report them to their guidance counselor, tell your administration, and call the parents.

You will probably witness fights at school. Your main job during these incidents is to protect yourself and your students while trying to alleviate the situation as quickly as possible. Each school district has its own rules concerning how you should handle a fight, so make sure that you consult with other teachers and administrators before such events occur.

You are not likely to witness major incidents of school violence but this does not mean that you should be unprepared. Make sure that you are intimately aware of your role in your school's emergency plans.

Beat Bullying 80

Bullying occurs at most schools. It is key that the administration and teachers come up with a consistent policy for preventing, identifying, and dealing with bullies. Following are some things that schools have done:

- Teachers include information about bullying in the curriculum.
- Schools work on increasing community awareness through pamphlets and other means.
- Guidance counselors and others make themselves available for students to talk about bullying.
- Schools that have bullying problems increase supervision in areas such as the lunchroom, the playground, and the parking lot.
- Administrators work with the entire staff, dealing with sensitivity to victims and their families so they can truly help the bullied victims.

If you notice that certain students are often a target, pull them aside and give them some techniques that might help them deal with the situation. Often, simply agreeing with bullies or laughing at what they are saying will defuse the situation. Once an individual is no longer seen as an easy target, he will more than likely be left alone as the bully moves on to others who they feel can be overpowered.

81 Expect (and Plan for) the Unexpected

Your first order of business as a teacher is to expect the unexpected. Realize that things will probably not go as you planned. Situations will arise that will test your patience and require extra effort on your part. If you find yourself without a classroom, in an overcrowded classroom, or with no textbooks, this is definitely not the ideal way to begin teaching. However, you should still realize that you can have an effective year of teaching if you use common sense and follow the principles described in this book.

Your reaction and success depends on your attitude and the way you face each new situation. Actively look for ways to improve your situation at every turn. Do not just assume there is nothing you can do. Instead, work with what you do have to create a good experience for yourself and your students. If you do not believe that you can work under the conditions set before you, then you will be right. Similarly, if you believe that you can make it through the year, you will be right too.

Cope with Too Few Textbooks?

Many school districts are facing budget crunches, and textbooks are often where schools and districts cut costs. You may find that you have fewer books than you have students. You will not be able to send books home which means that you will not be able to assign readings from the book as homework. If you are lucky, you will have enough books to create a class set. If you are not so lucky, you will not have any textbooks at all.

Class Sets

Class sets of textbooks are common in classrooms across the United States. Texts are very expensive and schools rarely purchase texts for more than a few classes in any given year. Many districts may choose to spend less on texts leaving one set for each teacher's students to share.

Class sets can pose real problems for teachers in terms of record keeping and organization. Teachers have to devise systems for keeping track of their books at all times. If a student has been sick, teachers have to arrange for them to check out a text for the evening to make up work. Unfortunately, if a teacher only has exactly the number of texts he needs for his classes, he may not even be able to let a student take a book for the evening.

83 Teach with No Textbooks—If You Have to

Worse than a class set situation is one where you have no textbooks at all. While this will most likely happen because of budget constraints, there are some schools that frown on textbook use completely. Some administrators feel that texts lend themselves to a lecture and busy-work mentality. By removing textbooks, they hope that teachers will turn to other more creative methods of content delivery.

This situation can be really hard for the new teacher. It is one thing for a teacher who has many years' experience teaching a course to be told they will no longer have a textbook. It is another for a novice to be presented with this situation. They often do not have the time or energy to create their own curriculum in the beginning. In most cases, they are still trying to figure out how to best deal with student disruptions and organization issues.

If you are placed in this situation, find yourself a good textbook to use as your guide even if you do not use it with your students. Try to get your school to purchase supporting material and ready-made lessons to help you get through the year. Keep your eye out for anything that you might find useful. Lesson ideas can come from the strangest places. If you have real concerns about your lack of text, talk to your mentor or other veteran teachers. Many times, teachers will have old lessons and worksheets that you can adapt for your classroom situation.

Deal with Outdated and Inaccurate Texts

Sometimes the textbooks you have to use are so old that the information is inaccurate or obsolete. For example, if your school has not replaced its geography books since the breakup of the Soviet Union, you really cannot effectively teach about that part of the world using the book. Therefore, you will need to supplement this information with material from magazines, news sites, and other books to give your students the correct information. Unfortunately, this can mean extra work for you. When you do need to supplement a text because it is outdated, keep your lessons simple.

Textbooks are written by humans, who can make mistakes. Textbook writers and editors also have personal biases that make it into the texts. Furthermore, interest groups and influential states can have a huge impact on what is and what is not included in a text. All of this means that you need to make sure and read the text critically before you create assignments for students. This ensures that you are not reinforcing inaccurate or biased information. As you move through your teaching career, an interesting assignment may be for students to examine certain pages or chapters in their texts for inaccuracies or bias.

85 Overcome Overcrowded Classrooms

Overcrowding at schools is almost a given in most areas of the country. Even though the school you work for might publish a fairly good teacher-to-student ratio, this number is usually inaccurate in terms of what really happens in the classrooms around campus. There are many teachers who have very small or no classes. For example, there might be a special education co-teacher who is in classes all day long with another teacher. This counts as two teachers in the room and therefore reduces the overall number of students for each teacher in the school.

Even worse, some schools count people who would not traditionally be thought of as teachers. For example, if a guidance counselor also has a few student aides, the counselor might be counted as a teacher for the purposes of the ratio. This is not to say that counselors are not teaching their student aides important skills. However, it does give an inaccurate picture of school loads. What ends up happening in this situation is that fewer full-time teaching positions are offered, saving the school district money while still allowing them to report better student-teacher ratios.

86 Manage the Room Even When You Are Outnumbered

If you are faced with thirty-five or forty kids in a class, you will find that many problems are magnified by overcrowding. What would be minor discipline issues in smaller classrooms can quickly escalate because of the number of students in the class.

More than in any other situation, you need to have a firm hand when it comes to discipline in an overcrowded classroom. You cannot allow this type of class to get out of control because getting them back on task can be nearly impossible. Make sure that you strictly follow your discipline plan as you teach each day.

Closely following your discipline plan does not mean that you will no longer be friendly with your students. It is important that you do not make them feel as if they are to blame for the overcrowding or that they are unwanted. Use your own sense of humor and don't forget to smile even when you feel as though want to scream.

You will also want to be doubly sure that your classroom management systems are efficient. Your restroom use policy, late work guidelines, and makeup work system should be clear and easy to use for you and the students or you will be spending a lot of each day dealing with these issues.

87 Tailor Lessons to a Large Class

Large classes make interesting assignments like debates and simulations more challenging. Therefore, think about the logistics of an activity before you put it in your lesson plan. Place careful limits on each of these types of activities you attempt.

Further, you will want to make clear rules concerning class discussions. Many teachers become lax when it comes to making students raise their hands to make comments. However, with a large group such as this, it is imperative that you have students raise hands to be recognized simply to keep order.

Finally, realize that you have to grade whatever you assign. The difference between grading twenty and forty essays can be huge. This does not mean that you should shirk your teaching duties to lessen your workload. However, it does mean that you should try to avoid placing grading-intensive assignments right after each other. Plan to give yourself a break every once in a while.

When you are grading time-consuming assignments, make sure to rely on tools like rubrics and peer grading. The more organized you are when you make your assignment to the students, the more likely they will give you their work in a format that makes your grading easier.

Dispersing Kids When There Are Too Few Desks

Overcrowded classrooms lead to a shortage of desks for students. As previously stated, you should not make students feel uncomfortable for being in your classroom. Realize that the desk situation is a temporary one. For one thing, classes are often unbalanced during the first week or two of school, so you may lose some of the students to another class. Further, you may find that the teachers around you have smaller classes than you do, in which case they'll give you some of their desks.

Your administration will probably have a procedure for reporting if you do not have enough desks. However, if you have gone a couple of days into the school year and students are still sitting on the floor of your classroom, discuss this with your administrator. Remember, these kids will tell their parents, who will probably call and complain to the school about the situation. Even though you did not cause the situation, you might find that the parents do blame you. Therefore, be proactive and make sure that the office knows of your predicament. They will work out a solution.

89 Teach Different Level Classes—Multiple Preps

Teaching more than one subject in a term is known as having multiple preps. For example, you might be assigned to teach regular and advanced/honors biology requiring two different lesson plans.

Organization Is Key

Again, it is very important to stay organized. One idea is to use colored folders for each class. That way, you can tell without looking at the title of a file which class it is associated with. As soon as a piece of paper crosses your desk, categorize it and stick it in the correct folder.

Ask for Help

It should not embarrass you to ask for help. Asking for help can be as simple as discussing your problems with other teachers over lunch. Self-reliance is a great thing. However, those who truly make it do it by "standing on the backs of giants." If you happen to have multiple preps *and* float, realize that the ability to adapt is within you.

Do Not Reinvent the Wheel

A year in which you are given multiple preps is not the year to try all kinds of new things. Keep things simple so that you can actually have a life outside of school. Realize that you will probably not be the most creative teacher you can be because of your situation. However, you are learning important skills to help you in all classes and the future.

In Case of Emergency 90

Most of your teaching days will be fairly normal. You might have a few disruptions occur each day, but you will not have many incidents that completely stop education in your classroom or the school for extended periods of time.

However, large disruptions will occur. They can range from the harmless to the severe, which can include the following:

- Surprise fire and tornado drills
- Actual fires and tornadoes
- Bomb threats and scares
- Classroom and school-wide power outages
- Incidents of school violence
- Tragic loss of a student or teacher
- Tragic world events that affect the students
- School pranks and vandalism

This list is not meant to scare you. However, it is good to be aware of situations that might occur and to have an idea of how you should react. Most schools have established plans to deal with many of these issues. Make sure you have your attendance and grade book readily available because it will be a necessity during emergencies.

As a new teacher, you can look at facing the unexpected as a scary proposition or as a challenge waiting to be met. Your attitude will carry over into your day-to-day teaching. More importantly, it will influence your students in ways you cannot even imagine.

Part Six

Assessments, Grading, and Testing, Oh My!

Effective lessons need to be accompanied by authentic assessments—evaluations or tests that directly examine what students have learned. When students have successfully completed an authentic assessment, the teacher can feel confident that they have learned the major topics and ideas presented in the lessons. It takes a lot of work to create effective, authentic assessments and grade them in a fair and consistent fashion.

91 Make Sure Your Assessments Are on Point

Assessments should measure what you teach to the students. That might sound simplistic, but many times teachers who believe they have created valid assessments are disappointed with the results. For example, if your assignment questions or directions are confusing, then you might not get the results you expect.

Try to read through your questions from a student's point of view to catch any confusing points before you give the quiz or assignment. If the results are not as expected, do not be afraid to evaluate your assessment for validity. If you find that it was at fault, you could have the students complete a new assessment. Over time, you will get a real feel for what students will respond best to.

There are two types of assessments: norm-referenced and criterion-referenced. Norm-referenced assessments compare students against others who have already taken the tests. These are used most typically for standardized tests like the SAT. Students are compared to a reference group to determine how they rank. It is normally best to stay away from this type of practice in your classroom, especially if you are teaching lower grades.

On the other hand, criterion-referenced assessments measure how well students have learned the material. This is the most commonly used type of assessment that teachers use in the classroom. A benefit of this type of assessment is that it is possible for everyone who has learned the information to earn a passing grade.

Pretest to Know Where to Start 92

Assessments don't need to be limited to the period after a lesson. In fact, you may find it useful to test students before a lesson in order to see where they are. For example, if you are reviewing basic concepts at the beginning of algebra, assessing students first can help you find any weak points students might have.

Pretests can also give you a basis for knowing how much students actually master from your lessons. You can see if they have increased in knowledge and understanding when compared to posttests. Some teachers even base their students' grades on the amount of improvement between the pretests and post-tests.

If you follow this route, make sure you avoid using exactly the same questions on both tests. Students will eventually catch on that they can simply study exactly what was asked on the first test to do well on the second one. However, you should blend some of the same questions in with new ones to measure improvement and achievement. In the end, however, remember that a test is an imperfect instrument. You should use your own observations of student achievement and progression in combination with the results from these tests.

93 Recognize What Grades Really Mean

What is the purpose and meaning of grades? What is the difference in your mind between an A and a B? Should As be given only for mastering hard-to-learn concepts or information? You really need to look at these and many other questions before you begin grading students.

You may receive pressure from the administration about your grades. It is important that you maintain your own belief of what constitutes A-quality work. If a student comes back a few years after leaving your class, and he or she cannot read, people are going to question how he or she could possibly have received an A (or B or C) in your class.

On the other hand, you should realize that if you give an inordinate amount of Ds or Fs, you will probably receive a lot of questions from your administration. Some administrations actively discourage giving low grades to students, which can be difficult for a new teacher to fight. However, if you have a good reason to give low grades, and you have the evidence to prove that the student earned those grades, then you should definitely do it.

On a final note, if you give a test or assignment that every student fails, you should take a deeper look at the reasons. If something was confusing or there was a problem with the wording, you might want to consider throwing out the results. If it was caused by a lack of studying on your students' part, then definitely keep and use the scores.

94 Use Rubrics

Rubrics are an excellent way to grade assignments that are complicated or that would be difficult to grade objectively. Basically, a rubric lays out for the teacher what requirements each part of the assignment must meet to receive full or partial credit. Then, when a teacher is grading an assignment like an essay, they can read through the assignment and compare this with the rubric to determine what grade to give the students. Rubrics are an excellent way to make your life easier, while also letting students know exactly what is expected of them.

It is a good idea to present students with the rubric that you will use to grade their assignment when you first assign the work. This allows students to see exactly what you are going to be looking for as you grade. You can give the students a copy of the rubric or simply post it on the board or overhead projector.

Some teachers find it useful to actually have students grade their own work based on the rubric before they turn in their assignment. This does not mean that you will use this grade, but it helps the students focus on the quality of their own work.

One final use of rubrics is if you have students grading their peers. Unless you give the students a rubric from which to grade, they will not grade each other's work consistently.

95 Create Effective Rubrics

The most time-consuming part of working with rubrics is creating effective ones. This should be done before you assign the students their work.

Use the following to help guide your creation of rubrics.

1. List what you want your students to accomplish with the assignment.
2. Organize your list from most to least important.
3. Decide how much you want your assignment to be worth.
4. Assign each item from Step 2 a percentage value out of 100 percent.
5. Multiply your percentage value by the total value for the assignment to get the point value for each item.
6. Decide on specific grading criteria for each item.
7. Transfer this information into a chart with columns left blank for actual grade assigned and comments.
8. When you grade the assignment, use this form and attach it to the assignment.

As you can see, it is easier to grade if you know what categories you will be grading when you create your assignment. For example, if you are grading an essay, you might include the following categories in your rubric: thesis, points of evidence, concluding paragraph, overall quality, and grammar and spelling. Having a rubric to grade essays will result in more consistent and fair grading on your part.

96 Find Time to Grade

At times, keeping on top of grading can be a real challenge. For one thing, the short planning periods that teachers are given is usually not enough time to even begin grading all of the work that students turn in. This means that teachers spend a lot of their personal time grading work. No matter when you choose to grade your students' work, grading takes time, so it is important that you decide on some strategies to lessen your grading time.

Some people may think that if teachers devise ways to cut down on their grading time, they are adding to the problems of public education. But cutting down on grading time does not mean cutting down on the quality of the grading. It only means that as you devise assignments or decide on methods to grade, you should consider the consequences in terms of your own time. If you become overworked, then you will end up stressed and burnt out.

Many classes require students to write essays. However, essays can often be difficult and time-consuming to grade. It is important that you devise grading methods to make your life easier.

First, you should definitely create a rubric for each of your essays. Your rubric should be consistent from essay to essay, with only the details changed in accordance with each topic. Your rubric should be convenient for you to use, so spend some time making your expectations very clear.

97 Peer Grade/Edit—Helps Everyone Learn

You can also have students do some peer editing to cut down on grading time. In this situation, students would get in a group and grade each other's assignments using rubrics that you have created. This can be a very effective means of helping students learn to write better essays.

If you are going to do this, it is a good idea to assign students an identifying number, which they use on their paper in place of their names. Do not place a student's own work in the group. This helps cut down on students giving good or poor grades based on popularity.

Once a student is given back their work, they can go through and make corrections before submitting the assignment to you. While some groups of students may not respond to this type of assignment as well as others, others will find it very useful. If you are preparing students for Advanced Placement exams, this approach can be a great exercise to help them look at their own writing in a different light. You will still need to look over the students' grades, but much of your work will be done with this type of system.

Teach Academic Integrity—A Weighty Issue

98

You will be faced with integrity issues as you teach. The fact is that cheating is widespread. Students cheat off of each other or plagiarize work all the time. Some teachers choose to ignore this because the issue is difficult to deal with. However, if we truly want our students to be prepared, we must take a strong stand against cheating.

Develop Your Own Policy on Cheating

Most schools have discipline policies related to cheating. They usually state that students caught cheating will be awarded a zero for their work. It is your job to enforce this policy. It is not always easy to catch cheaters. While you might be able to catch someone looking at another student's paper during a test, it is much harder to catch someone who has an old copy of a test.

Therefore, it is a good idea for you to vary your tests from year to year. If you have a real problem, you can even vary them from class to class. If you are having an issue with students cheating during tests, surprise them with different forms of tests.

Sometimes catching cheaters seems like a losing proposition. Students are not easy to catch and are often very defensive when you do catch them. Parents sometimes have a hard time believing their children have cheated. However, if you believe in the integrity of the school system, then you have to keep trying.

99 Avoid and Deal with Plagiarism

Plagiarism is a specialized form of cheating whereby students and others directly copy words or unique ideas from other sources. Sometimes students mistakenly plagiarize because they do not understand all the rules. For example, it is considered plagiarism to copy an entire encyclopedia entry and then simply include a citation at the end. However, students feel that since they cite their source, they have not plagiarized. It's important to teach your students exactly what plagiarism is and is not before they begin working on any research projects.

It can often be difficult to catch students who have plagiarized. For one thing, it is often difficult to find the original source. This is where the Internet can help. Type a unique part of the suspected plagiarized work into a search engine to see if you come up with any exact matches. Special software to help teachers catch plagiarized text is also available.

However, if students have used printed materials that have not been transferred online or are not listed on search engines, then you will have a hard time finding the source. When this occurs, you will have to rely on methods such as comparing the writing structure of the student's normal work to that of the suspected passage. If there are big words in the passage, you could ask the student to define the word for you. You could even ask him to explain what he has written in his own words.

None of this is an exact science. It is a sad fact that students can go online and buy research papers. Technically, this isn't plagiarism, and it's hard to catch. Your school and you personally must have a staunch policy against such work. If it is found that a student bought a research paper, for example, from a paper mill, then this needs to be punished according to a set policy.

There will be some students who "get away with it" without your knowledge. Therefore, your best defense for catching plagiarism and cheating might be a good offense. Consider requiring an oral defense of all research papers to be presented in front of the class. After the presentation, you could ask questions about specific parts of their paper. Even if students buy their papers, they will still have to master the material in order to answer your questions.

Realize that students will try and cheat. Even some of the best students will be tempted when high stakes are on the line. When the difference between valedictorian and salutatorian is extremely little, then students might turn to these types of activities.

101 Understand the Purpose of High-Stakes Testing

Tests that bear major consequences have been around for a long time. In China during the Tang Dynasty (A.D. 618–906), civil service exams were widely used as a way to combat the practice of patronage by rewarding people with government jobs based on what they knew, not whom they knew. This merit system was a huge improvement for its time. United States civil service exams are based on these ancient tests.

High-stakes testing is descended from these exams. It is a practice that relates success on a standardized test to rewards of one kind or another. Conversely, failing a high-stakes test usually has adverse consequences. Examples of consequences include being held back in a grade or not being allowed to graduate until the test is passed. For schools, consequences for failure might mean lower levels of funding or in extreme cases school closure. High-stakes testing has a long history and it is still widely used in the United States today for many reasons including increasing educator accountability and ensuring that students are achieving at a minimum level.

102 Get to Know the State of Education Today

According to the No Child Left Behind Act of 2001, states are required to administer academic assessments of students in grades four and eight for reading and math. States may also choose to conduct assessments of reading and math in grade twelve. This reinforces the trend that more states are instituting standardized tests, many of which at least partially determine funding for schools and graduation eligibility.

Proponents of this act claim that with more standardized testing, there will be greater teacher accountability concerning student learning. Further, it is believed that if students are at least proficient enough to pass the exams, then they have received a basic, sound education. Opponents of the plan, on the other hand, feel that it is inappropriate to put so much weight on one exam. They often feel that test bias or test anxiety can adversely affect scores and therefore render the tests inaccurate.

While politicians and educational leaders continue arguing over this issue, day-to-day teachers have little control over what goes. As a teacher, your only option is to make the best of the decisions that are handed down to you.

103 Realize What's at Stake

As already indicated, many state exams have consequences for students, teachers, and schools. While some states have chosen not to tie graduation to the passing of an exam, others have or are intending to implement such a program. Further, many states now base at least a portion of school funding on student test performance. Thus, those involved have much at stake.

Standardized testing in and of itself is not a bad idea. It is definitely better to reward someone for their merit as opposed to their personal connections. However, high-stakes standardized testing must be based on the body of knowledge students actually learn in order to be valid. Unfortunately, even the best tests require that students spend extra time on test preparation—which means less time spent on learning.

The sad fact is that on average, students from lower socioeconomic backgrounds score lower on standardized tests. Sometimes these students do not receive the same level of education in their schools. Also, it is often argued that they do not have as much practice taking standardized tests or that the tests may be biased against them. The belief among opponents of high-stakes testing is that the pressure of these types of tests can be harmful to these and other disadvantaged students.

Plan for High-Stakes Testing

In many states, schools are also heavily affected by the results of standardized testing. For example, in the state of Florida, each school is given a grade on a scale from A to F. The school's grade is based on many standards, including how its students achieved and improved on the FCAT. Schools that achieve high grades earn financial rewards.

Additionally, when a school first earns an F, it gets decreased state aid. However, if the school continues to receive low grades, the state may intervene. One of the effects of this intervention is to provide students with vouchers called Opportunity Scholarships. These scholarships allow the students to choose a different public school or to receive the cost of their public education for one year to help pay for a private school of their choice.

Obviously, the stakes in this type of atmosphere make high achievement on the FCAT a top priority. In fact, at least one high school in Florida has offered students money for passing the various portions of the FCAT. The opinions of state politicians on this situation were varied. Even though the students who achieved the passing scores probably liked the "reward," one has to question whether this does not send the wrong message to students.

105 Find What's Good about Standardized Tests

There are many people who believe that high-stakes standardized testing is a necessary element of our educational system. Following are some of the cited benefits:

Holding Educators Accountable

Some people believe that teachers are to blame for the problems in education today. Low pay, the effects of tenure, and the loosening of certification requirements has meant that some teachers are just not very good. Proponents of standardized high-stakes testing feel that the system forces teachers to cover at least a minimum of quality information for students.

Providing Measures for Comparison

Typically, parents rely on word of mouth and rumors labeling schools as good or bad based on others' perceptions. Proponents of high-stakes testing claim that these tests allow the public a means for comparing schools.

Further, by exposing disparities between schools, more assistance can be given to those schools that most need it.

Increasing Student Motivation

Student motivation is another important point cited by proponents of high-stakes testing. Because these tests are required for promotion and/or graduation, students have a real motivating factor for achievement.

See What's Not Good about Standardized Tests

Even as proponents cite important benefits for the implementation of high-stakes testing, opponents claim that there are reasons to support its elimination. Some say:

Tests Do Not Mirror Curriculum

Many people argue that current standardized tests do not test what students are actually supposed to be learning in their courses. Teachers have to stop teaching their required curriculum in order to spend time getting students ready to pass the tests. They test "artificial" information that does not truly show student achievement.

Undue Pressure

Opponents often argue that high-stakes testing puts too much pressure on students and teachers. They claim that students can actually be harmed by the amount of emphasis placed on passing these exams. This is especially true for students with learning disabilities. This pressure, they argue, actually results in less—not more—learning.

Standardized Testing Is Biased

People who believe that high-stakes testing is a bad practice also cite the bias that appears to be inherent in standardized testing. Minority students and those from lower-income families get lower scores, on average, on these tests. Therefore, using them as a method for comparison between schools is not valid and is actually harmful.

107 Know How the Tests Affect You

You will be affected by standardized testing in one way or another. Since students across the nation are being required to take these tests, you will probably spend time addressing the information to be tested or actually delivering the exams. If the tests have high-stakes issues associated with them, then you will be subject to even greater pressure.

Standardized tests that students must pass to graduate will get a lot of attention. If you are teaching juniors or seniors, you will probably be required to spend at least some time directly preparing students for their exam. If a lot of students fail these exams, questions will be asked of their school and their teachers. People will want to know why they were not prepared. Instructors who teach in grades where the tests affect student promotion will also face similar pressure.

However, teachers are under the greatest pressure when funding is tied to results of standardized tests. In these instances, teachers in all grades are pushed to spend time preparing students for their exams. If the tests mirror the curriculum students are to learn anyway, this is not a major burden. However, if the opposite is true, then teachers might find they spend more time preparing students for the test than teaching their own courses. Teachers in this situation must make the best of it. They should not spend time complaining to the students about the worthiness of the exam. This could have the adverse affect because students might not take it seriously.

Teach to the Test? 108

Is teaching to the test a bad thing? The answer depends on the test in question. If it's a well-constructed test that actually measures what a person should have learned, teaching to the test is a good idea. In other words, teaching to the test in this case would mean teaching exactly what the students should be learning through the curriculum. Aside from a few days of specific preparation for the test questions, teachers would not have to make major changes to their lessons. In fact, this might get teachers who would not otherwise have taught some important parts of the curriculum to include them in their lessons.

On the other hand, if the test in question is poorly constructed, and it does not measure what students should have learned, then teaching to the test means that educators are not teaching students what they need to know. Instead of following the state and national standards, teachers might only include information relevant to the test. This is especially true when the stakes involved are high. Therefore, these students might become excellent at taking Test XYZ, but they will fail to master the required subjects in school.

Testing is not inherently bad. However, the factors must align so that teachers are forced to teach according to the state and national standards. Students must be tested on the information that they should have learned in the first place. Only when this occurs will "teaching the curriculum" and "teaching to the test" mean the same thing.

Part Seven

Technology and Online Learning Today

Some schools put a lot of emphasis on technology; others may be unable to come up with the funds necessary to purchase computer hardware and software. Technology at times has been viewed as the savior of public education. However, technology is not a solution in and of itself. Presented or used improperly, technology in the classroom may prove to be ineffective, a costly way of wasting valuable teaching time.

109 Look at the Disparity Among School Funds

The technological disparity among schools and districts is staggering. Some school districts provide a great deal of funds to buy technology for schools. Many schools across the country are wired for broadband technology, which provides them with high-speed access to the Internet. Some even have wireless access for all their students. However, there are also many school districts that do not have enough funds to provide more than a handful of computers to their schools. This disparity only exacerbates the problems in education. In fact, it can often act as a lightning rod for criticism.

The sad fact is that many of the schools that do not have a lot of technology are located in the poorest areas of town. Since computers and technology have become such an integral part of the world around us, it is imperative that we do not create a situation where some students are left behind because of where they live. With this said, it is also important that we do not rob important programs like the arts for the funds to purchase additional technology.

Make and Suggest Smart Purchases 110

Many schools do not spend enough time researching or planning their technology purchases. They often lack an overall plan for technology, and there is a belief that buying any technology is better than no technology at all. They often end up purchasing items that are a "good deal" but that might not really be useful in the classroom. Sometimes, these purchases are just too difficult to integrate. Other times, they are incompatible with systems already in place.

What schools need is a well-thought-out plan to buying new technology. Teachers should be an integral part of the planning process. They will be the ones actually using the purchased technology in their classrooms. Because many new teachers know more about the available technology than veteran teachers, it may be a good idea for you to join the technology committee. By helping to develop a workable purchasing plan, you'll make sure you have the technological tools that will make your teaching experience more efficient and effective. With that said, make sure that you do not step on the toes of older staff members with your "knowledge." Try to be helpful and work with the team.

111 Use Technology the Right Way

An important question that all schools need to answer is, "What is the purpose of technology in our school?" Will technology solve the major problems facing the school? Will it raise student achievement levels? What impact will it have?

The truth is that technology is not the panacea for all of education's ills. It is simply a tool that effective teachers can use to help reinforce and teach important concepts. It is not the end of education—it is just the beginning.

If teachers rely too heavily on technology without a clear picture of how it should be integrated into their lessons, students may miss out on important parts of the educational process. If a teacher simply sends students to the computer lab each day to work on a computer program, they are not truly teaching. While some programs do provide accountability measures, most do not.

Even in the case of online courses, experience has found that only if a real teacher is an integral part of the educational process do the courses reach their full potential. Similarly, teachers who simply use technology without trying to determine the best method of use within the framework of their class will not see many benefits.

Make Lessons Better with Computers

112

Many excellent computer games, simulations, and programs exist to support your education in the classroom. Manufacturers usually have demonstrations that you can go through to get a feel for these programs before ordering them. Realize that when you buy a single copy of a software program, it is meant for personal use. If you plan on using a program with a whole class, your school needs to purchase it for each student or buy a site license that allows unlimited use of a program.

The main problem that teachers will face once they get programs that are effective educational aids is the logistics of setting up these programs for practice. Some schools provide computer labs, and teachers are allowed to sign up in advance and take their students there during a class period. This allows each student to have access to a computer. If your school does not have enough computers at the computer lab, then you might have to assign groups of students to share computers. You might also need to space out the use of the program over several days, which often results in lost classroom time for other projects and lessons.

113 Learn to Monitor Their Online Learning

The rise of the Internet has changed many different parts of our lives, from shopping to education. Students are turning more and more frequently to the Internet for research. However, there are many issues and problems associated with the Internet that you and your students need to be aware of.

Offensive Sites

One of the foremost concerns many parents have is what their children are accessing on the Internet. Some schools place restrictive software on their computers to limit the types of sites that students can visit. However, this is not always the best solution because both offensive and inoffensive sites can be blocked. Further, there are some legal questions concerning their constitutionality in terms of free speech.

The alternative to restrictive software is the creation of strict acceptable-use policies for students and teachers. Students who are caught accessing pornographic or otherwise offensive sites are subject to punishment. It is important to remember that if students access these types of sites in your presence or during your class, you may be called to answer questions from parents or administrators.

114 Watch What and Who You Trust

Another issue that often arises with the use of the Internet is the quality of the information that is accessed. While there is a lot of excellent information available, there is also a lot of inaccurate and potentially dangerous material accessible to students. Further, most articles on the Internet are biased according to their author's point of view. It is very important that you and your students learn to discriminate between good and bad sites along with determining what prejudices the authors might have.

When evaluating Web sites, you and your students will want to ask the following questions:

- Is the author listed, and can you read his or her biographical information?
- Is the Web site associated with a product or sponsored by a particular interest group?
- Is the information dated? Does it say when the site was last updated?
- Does the author cite any resources?

The quality of the sources that students use should be an integral part of the grading process.

115 Integrate Technology Effectively

In order to effectively and seamlessly integrate technology into your classroom, you must be very familiar with its operation. Do not present a computer program to students that you have not practiced using first. Without this initial experience, technology will always be awkward and will take more time than it is worth.

You should have an alternative lesson ready whenever you use technology, in case there's a glitch. If you are using the Internet, your connection might be down. If you are using a computer program, something could have happened to corrupt the disk. In other words, make sure that you are prepared in case the worst scenario happens. Do not lose precious teaching time by failing to have another lesson prepared.

There are many activities that you can do with the technology that is available today. Research has been made so much richer with the advent of the Internet. It used to be that students were limited to the books and periodicals available at their school or local libraries. Now they have so many more interactive options available to them.

Find Other Options If Your School Can't Afford Much

Not all schools can afford purchasing the most up-to-date technology. Without having to dig deep into your own pockets, how can you bring new technology into your school?

Government and Private Grants

Government agencies and private industries often advertise technology grants that teachers and schools can apply for. Remember, when you apply for a grant, you include a proposal for how the award will be used. If you get awarded the grant, you must show your progress toward your stated goal, which does require record keeping and further effort on your part.

Other Alternatives

You can also try a more grassroots effort for buying technology. Why not organize a fundraiser to buy software programs or computers?

Visit local businesses and try to get them to sponsor classrooms. They may be willing to aid in the purchase of computers or programs. They may even donate items that could be useful, like keyboards or mouses. Then you could have the school newspaper recognize their contribution. If you can get the community behind your effort, then technology can become an integral part of your educational strategy.

117 Determine How Valid Is Virtual Education Is

Online education can take many forms ranging from the traditional idea of distance learning to something much more teacher-driven. The most effective method of online education is the teacher-driven mode.

In this model, students receive content and turn in assignments through the Internet. However, they have a teacher for each course who stays in close contact through phone calls, discussions boards, online chats, and e-mail messages. Students are able to work whenever they want. Teachers have the flexibility to set their own hours during the day, since they too work from home.

Online or virtual education is only about ten years old, so it is really still in its infancy. Each year, numerous online schools emerge as educators and politicians realize the potential of online learning. One of the constants of online education today is change. Because technology and information are changing so rapidly, the state of online education is continuously in flux. However, one thing is certain: Online learning is here to stay.

Online Teaching Jobs

Each year the number of jobs offered by virtual schools greatly increases. Some schools such as FLVS (see facing page) have part-time opportunities for educators who wish to become involved in this exciting form of teaching. While teaching online is not for everyone, it does provide many benefits and can be a rewarding career.

Look at a Case Study: The Florida Virtual School

The Florida Virtual School is a leader in online education. The school was awarded the Excellence in Distance Learning Programming, Pre-K–12 Education award in 2000, 2002, and 2003 by the United States Distance Learning Association. This accredited program provides a wide range of courses for middle and high school students.

When students sign up for courses, they are also assigned a teacher who helps them out every step of the way. In fact, the hands-on role of the teacher is something that truly makes the FLVS work. Teachers make monthly phone calls, create monthly progress reports, and are always available to answer questions through e-mail and over the phone.

FLVS prides itself on the level of parental involvement in each student's education. By talking each month to both the students and their parents, educators gain a real partner whose sole goal is to help their child succeed. This is something that sets FLVS apart from other education providers.

The motto of FLVS is, "Any time, any place, any path, any pace." What this means is that students have a variety of choices to help them take control of their education. Further, teachers work hard with students to create individualized learning programs. While students do have deadlines to meet as they complete courses, they also have a huge amount of flexibility that is not afforded them in traditional schools. As long as they have an Internet connection available, students can work on their courses.

119 Consider Online Learning—the Way of the Future?

While it is not likely that online education will ever completely replace the traditional classroom, quality education over the Internet will continue to grow and develop until it is a viable alternative for all students.

Crowded Schools and Teacher Shortages

School crowding is a nationwide epidemic. Many school districts do not have the money to keep up with growing populations of students. They just cannot afford to build enough schools. Consequently, schools become overcrowded. Some turn to solutions like double sessions—half the student body goes to school in the morning and half in the afternoon—but this situation is not in anyone's best interest. Combine overcrowding with a shortage of qualified teachers, and you have a problem of epic proportions. Online education can truly help this situation.

A Lack of Choices

While many schools provide students with a wide range of curriculum choices, others have little more than the core curriculum courses. Many rural schools are actually "undercrowded" and experience teacher shortages. These schools find it difficult to offer a broad range of classes and may not have any Advanced Placement courses at all. Online education can help fill in the gaps.

Watch for Special Opportunities

Many students who have learning disabilities find that online education affords them greater flexibility for completion and achievement. In a classroom setting, a teacher might present information for fifty minutes, leaving some students behind; online, students control how long it takes them to go through a lesson.

Unique Situations

Online learning has had a huge impact on those students caught in special situations in which a traditional school simply does not work. For example, sick and homebound students are able to take courses without leaving their homes. Students who have psychological problems such as agoraphobia (a fear of crowds) can still learn the curriculum while building relationships with others in a safe, online environment.

Students who are excellent athletes or who are working as actors, actresses, or entertainers and who are not home very often find online learning to be a wonderful alternative to tutors. These students can log on from wherever they are traveling and complete their work. They can participate in discussions with their instructors and other students to help them feel connected to a school even when they do not have one in the traditional sense. Further, their curriculum is standardized so they are not receiving less of an education than their peers at a traditional school setting.

121 Is Online Instruction for You?

The mind of an online instructor works completely differently from a traditional teacher's. For one thing, it has to be much more flexible. Whereas in a traditional classroom all students are basically in the same place at the same time, in the online environment students are all over the board. One student might be working in an early unit while another is just about done with their coursework. This does take some getting used to, but remember that it is better for students because it does not force them all to conform to the same schedule with the attitude of, "If they don't get it, it's their loss."

Online teaching is much more individualized. Students and teachers get to know each other very well through phone calls. While most online schools have schedules that students have to follow in order to keep them moving through the course, there is much more room for flexibility. If students start the year late, they are not considered behind. They do not have to "make up" work and "catch up" with the other students. They start on the schedule and follow it the same as the other students. In other words, the schedule is fitted to the student, not the student to the schedule.

Think about the Advantages 122

Online instructors have many benefits. Imagine never having to deal with tardies, absences, disruptions, school violence, fire drills, or even getting up in the morning and driving to work. These benefits are huge and cannot be overestimated. But precisely because it allows for so much freedom, online teaching requires a lot of self-discipline.

Another surprising benefit of online instruction is that it allows you to really get to know your students, sometimes even better than in the traditional classroom. The reason for this is that a normal class might consist of thirty students. If a teacher sees a class for only fifty minutes each day, it is impossible to truly connect with each and every student—there is just not enough time. However, online learning provides one-on-one learning opportunities as teachers call and talk to their students. There is an opportunity to get to know them as people and not just pupils in your classroom.

Parents can also become much more involved in their kids' education through an online learning environment. Many schools provide parents with access to their children's work and send them monthly progress reports. Teachers are usually required to call and talk to parents at least once a month. Many traditional school parents never hear from their students' teachers the entire year!

123 Realize the Issues for Online Teachers

Just as there are many benefits to online teaching and learning, there are also some issues that teachers need to be aware of. First, many people have a hard time adjusting to teaching from home. While working at home, you have to show a great sense of self-control so that you actually do your work. Further, you will not be interacting with "live" people each day—instead, you'll be working online or talking on the phone.

It is much harder to separate work life from home life when you work at home. Work can easily consume an inordinate amount of time, thereby leading to family issues and problems. While you can leave the traditional classroom at the end of the day, your work is always with you at home. Students are constantly e-mailing and turning in work. Knowing when to turn off the computer takes just as much self-discipline as knowing when to turn it on.

Finally, just as in traditional schools, you will be asked from time to time to perform extra duties. It is important to keep in mind that many of these extra duties will probably be completed during your own time. This means that your work schedule can quickly eat into your "life schedule." Make sure to keep your priorities straight, and you will be a much happier person and employee.

Can You Handle the Commitment? 124

Online learning does require a huge time commitment from the teacher, in a different way than in the traditional classroom. While online teachers do not necessarily work more hours than traditional teachers, they do have a very different schedule. This can make them feel like they are working more than in the regular classroom. One reason for this is that because students can work any time, they can ask questions any time. Therefore, you will probably need to check e-mail and voice messages every day of the week, including weekends.

Further, the students who go to traditional school will not be available for phone calls and other communication during normal working hours. Therefore, you will be making many phone calls in the evenings and on weekends.

Finally, online schools like FLVS do not close for typical holidays like the summer and winter breaks. Students will be continuing to work during these periods and you will be expected to teach. Since students are working at their own pace, they are able to take classes anytime during the year which provides much greater flexibility and continuity for them but means a less traditional schedule for you.

125 Catch Cheaters Even If You're Not There

One final concern that many online teachers have involves cheating. Just as in the traditional classroom, online cheating does occur. Because teachers are not seeing their students complete their exams or work in class, it is difficult to be assured that the work turned in is truly their own. That is where phone calls come into play. Online teachers must use phone calls to verify the knowledge of their students. During these phone calls, they can ask students about particular assignments or give them short oral quizzes to test their knowledge.

Online instructors also have the tools of the Internet at their disposal to help determine whether something has been plagiarized. If you think that a student has directly copied something, you can copy and paste the sentence into a search engine, like *www.google.com*, and see if any direct matches come up. Of course, this will not help for work that has been copied from written texts, but it does help control plagiarism issues. There are also pay services that your online school might choose to purchase which allows a greater ability to test for plagiarism.

Be Successful as an Online Instructor

In the end, success in online teaching is no different from success in the traditional classroom. Teachers must make policies that they stick to and create a positive, warm learning environment. Just because teachers are not directly seeing their students does not mean that they cannot convey their high expectations through comments and phone calls. An important benefit of online learning is that teachers can truly work to meet the needs of each individual student in a way that they could not in the traditional classroom.

Phone Calls

Phone calls are probably the most important part of having a successful career as an online instructor. When teachers do not call their students each month, they will find that some students actually work less or stop working altogether. They will feel disconnected.

Staying Flexible

Just as with the traditional classroom, an essential quality of an effective teacher is flexibility. Even more than in the traditional classroom, online teachers have to accept and embrace change and uncertainty. They have to be willing to have students starting at different times during the year. They have to be willing to make special allowances for certain students. They also have to understand that the Internet is a continually changing environment, and they might have to adjust to new teaching platforms.

Part Eight

Stress, Illness, and Substitutes

Much is expected of you as a teacher. With the daily demands on your time, it is no wonder that health concerns often fall by the wayside. Stress is a rampant problem among teachers. However, you cannot be an effective teacher if you aren't in good health—or if you aren't a happy and satisfied person. Teacher burnout is a common cause for teachers leaving the profession each year. Therefore, it's important that you take steps to combat illness and stress in order to excel in the rewarding field of teaching while keeping your sanity.

127 Avoid Getting Sick

Each year, teachers are exposed to many new germs. Every time a paper is handed in or a student borrows one of your pencils, you will be exposed to germs. It's very likely that younger students who haven't learned proper hygiene and manners will sneeze or cough close to you without covering their mouth. If you have a shared computer, then you are also subject to further exposure. In fact, just opening your door can cause you to get sick if the handle happens to hold germs to which you are not resistant.

New teachers are especially vulnerable to this. In most cases, the new teacher's body is simply not immune to all of the germs it will encounter. As a new teacher, you should expect to probably take all of the sick days you have available to you. Over time, you will build up a resistance to this and as the years go on will get sick less often. However, there are some steps you can take from the beginning to keep yourself and your students healthier.

Take Preventative Measures

Make sure that you wash your hands often and use anti-bacterial hand wash during class. Have this type of hand sanitizer available for student use. If students in your class are sneezing or coughing a lot, make sure that when they leave the classroom you clean their desks and the door handle along with anything else they might have touched. If it is the cold and flu season, and all your students seem to be catching the latest bug, you might consider avoiding assignments that require them to work in close groups. You should also make sure to take a daily multivitamin and to drink plenty of fluids. Healthy eating habits lead to better overall health.

Teaching Students to Be Thoughtful

Even though you are not your students' parent, you should still take some time to reinforce important life skills and manners. Whenever a student does not cover her mouth, point it out and tell her it is not acceptable. Make a point to discuss healthy behavior with your whole class as you enter flu season. While you will not always have a huge impact, you might get students to think more about the consequences of their actions.

129 Be Your Own Substitute

There is nothing shameful about staying home when you are really sick. However, there will be times when you are definitely not at your best but still not sick enough to stay home and use a sick day. These are the days when you need to learn to be your own best sub. This is one of the most valuable pieces of advice that you can receive.

Being your own best sub means that you are not going to put a ton of energy into your lesson for the day. It's fine to let students know that you are not feeling the best and that you expect them to behave while they do their assigned work. You might have the students copy notes, watch a pertinent and educationally sound movie, or give the students worksheets to complete in class. Of course this is not the way you should typically run your classroom. However, it is perfectly acceptable to do this every once in a while. Even on days when you are "subbing" for yourself, students will achieve more educationally than on days when actual subs are running your class.

130 If You Get Hurt on the Job

Getting hurt on the job is a daily occurrence in schools across the nation. It is important that if you get hurt, you take full advantage of the worker's compensation laws and know your rights. You need to protect yourself, so make sure that you fully understand the procedures and that you follow through.

Reporting Injuries

The first thing you must do in order to qualify for worker's compensation is to report your injury to your school. You will probably have to fill out an accident report describing exactly what happened. You should do this even if you think your injury is minor or you are not planning to visit a doctor. The reason for this is that if something related to your injury arises once you get home or over the next few days, you will be protected and covered. Sometimes injuries that seem minor worsen over time.

Most often, your school will send you to a doctor who handles the district's worker's compensation cases. Make sure that if you have any questions at all about the extent of your injury that you go see this doctor. Read up on your rights concerning second opinions and understand exactly what you should expect from the school if you require extensive medical attention or time away from the classroom.

131 Recognize a Sick Building When You See One

Just being present at some schools can cause health problems. This is because some school buildings are actually "sick" themselves. This means that dangerous pathogens are afloat in the air and can cause sickness through inhalation.

Likely Causes

Most of the time, a poor ventilation system is to blame for the problem. As dust builds up in ducts throughout the building, pathogens, mold spores, and other illness-causing molecules thrive. When this infectious dust begins circulating through the ventilation system, it becomes airborne.

How do you know if you are working in a sick building? There are many symptoms to watch for; if you see yourself or many of your fellow teachers experiencing the following, you should probably take some action.

- Frequent headaches
- Itchy, watery eyes
- Chronic fatigue
- Dizziness
- Problems with pregnancy
- Cough/sore throat
- Skin problems
- Nausea
- Cancer

Another good indicator to look out for is if you feel better when you spend time away from the building. Do the symptoms disappear over long breaks? If so, then they might be related to the building.

Take Action to Fix Your Facility

If you experience any of the above symptoms routinely, and you feel it is related to the building where you work, this should be reported. You should also notify your administration of any mold growths you notice in the school building. Unfortunately, it can be difficult for new teachers to take action. You may not be on a permanent contract and protected by tenure, and you may not want to make waves. It's also possible that you've heard horror stories about other teachers who reported problems and were subsequently transferred or fired.

However, your health should be your first concern. Record your symptoms over a period of time. If you notice mold growing in visible places, make sure that you take pictures of it. You can try to speak tactfully with your direct supervisor to see if anything happens. However, sometimes you might just have to go directly to the OSHA and the EPA to have them test the air quality. If you do this, others must join in your complaint.

If you can prove that you have been injured by the quality of the air, you are eligible to receive workman's compensation. Your school will also be required to make special accommodations for you under the Americans with Disabilities Act (ADA). You may even be given early retirement under certain circumstances. However, realize that it is often difficult to get a doctor to agree that the cause of your illness was definitely the building where you work.

133 Manage Stress on the Job

There are many causes of stress in a teacher's life—administrative red tape, student disruptions, noise, the demands of the job, and the personal pressure we as teachers put on ourselves each and every day. If you often have your heart pounding and feel like you are always on edge, then you are experiencing stress. Over time, this wears on your body and can cause you to be very sick. The effects of stress can lead to illness and even death, so it is not something to play around with.

External Factors That Cause Stress

External forces will cause most of the stress you will experience as a teacher. Often times you will feel like you're being pulled in many different directions. One of the biggest stresses for teachers comes with major changes in the school. It seems that some schools feel the need to make major changes each summer.

Another huge source of stress comes from the students themselves. Most students you will encounter will be very good. However, every year there will be at least one class that you dread. Often, the reason is one or a few students who give you grief—and if you do not have a good handle on discipline, the misbehaviors that arise will be very hard to take. Also remember that noise can lead to stress so work hard to enforce your rules and keep a quiet classroom.

134 Don't Be Too Hard on Yourself

Teacher burnout is a well-known event that happens to many teachers. Teachers are asked to do so much and are often the toughest on themselves. They expect a lot of themselves each and every day. If they do not feel that they are meeting the expectations of parents, students, the administration, the community, and themselves, then they might work themselves harder to try and succeed. However, pleasing everyone is just not possible.

As a teacher, if you never allow yourself to make a mistake or have an off day, you will eventually burn out. You must find a way to stay grounded as you go through the school year. Remember what is really important to you as you approach each day, teaching the students. The fact is that internal stressors are often the hardest to change so continue to be gentle and always send yourself positive messages.

135 Gain Relief from Stress

Stress relief begins and ends with your mind. You need to realize that you do not and cannot have control over every situation. Sometimes the administration will make choices that entirely change your work life. Unfortunately, you will not have any say in the matter. Students will misbehave in class, and even though you are in charge, you cannot always control these situations before they arise. The only thing that you can have complete control over is your own feelings and perceptions.

When stressful situations arise, choose to act and not react. Instead of sitting back and wallowing in misery, jump in and try to find ways to solve any problems or issues that arise. Even if you do not get your way in the end, just the act of getting involved will help you feel better.

Getting enough sleep, exercising, and practicing good eating habits are extremely important in fighting stress. Relaxation is the key to lower stress levels. When you feel that you're in a stressful situation, remember to breathe deeply. As you breathe in, scrunch up your entire body and then let it out at once; you will begin to relax.

Remember not to sweat the small stuff. While this may be an old cliché, it is still valid. When a stressful situation arises, consider if you will even remember it tomorrow or next week. The fact is that most situations are momentary.

Get Your Sleep

If you have ever been around a tired, cranky child, you know that sleep deprivation can seriously affect mood and attitude. Lack of sleep is a major cause of illness and stress for teachers and students alike. Sleep problems can lead to more mistakes and difficulty in concentrating. Make sure that you understand the symptoms of sleep deprivation, and take the time to get a good night's sleep each and every night.

If you struggle with sleep deprivation, you should try to keep regular hours and go to bed at the same time each night. If you constantly vary your bedtime, you will end up confusing your body. This can lead to further sleep problems.

Some ideas for helping you sleep better include avoiding caffeine, refraining from exercise just before going to bed, and finding some time to reflect on and write down things that have concerned you during the day.

Finally, if you just cannot get to sleep, it is best to get up and do something restful. Some people find that if they read, this will help them fall asleep more quickly. However, make sure that whatever you do, do not turn on bright lights. If you follow these steps, you should be well on your way to being a more rested and healthy person.

137 Give Substitutes a Fighting Chance

Substitutes have a very difficult job. They come into a classroom that they probably never visited before. They must control a class of thirty or more students who they probably have never met and do not know their names. While keeping the student's behavior under control, they also have to try and follow the lesson plan the teacher left behind. Therefore, keep this situation in mind as you create lesson plans and provide adequate information for your substitutes.

As everyone knows, students are prone to giving substitutes a very hard time. Students just do not feel the same need to behave and follow the rules with substitutes. Even the best students will often misbehave when a substitute is in charge. Your best chance to alleviate a possibly volatile situation is to create expectations for your students concerning their behavior. It is also imperative that you spend a lot of time providing information that will fully prepare your substitute for the situation.

Make a "Substitute Folder"

A substitute folder informs substitutes of your policies and procedures, and it allows them to communicate with you about the events of the day by leaving you notes and other papers in the substitute folder.

The Folder's Contents

Your substitute folder should be distinctive in color and have the words "Substitute Folder" written in large letters. What you choose to include in the folder is up to you. At a bare minimum, consider adding the following:

- Seating chart
- Discipline referrals
- Attendance sheets
- Daily class schedule
- Specific student information
- Hall passes
- Additional helpful notes
- Extra paper for the substitute teacher's comments to you

If you know that you will be out, you will want to leave your lesson in the folder. It is also a good idea to write the day's agenda on the board. This will give the substitute and students something to refer to during the class. It will also help cut down on confusion between the students and the substitute. Remember, a well-informed substitute is an effective substitute.

139 Plan for Productivity

If you want something productive to happen in your classroom when a substitute is present, you must leave a lesson plan. Just as you do when you create your own lesson plans, you must determine what you want students to learn while you are gone and how much they will finish in one class period. Generally, you should realize that students will not give substitute lessons as much credence as your own lessons. However, this should not keep you from having two or three important points that they should take away from the substitute's lesson. You can write these on the board before you leave or have the substitute write them at the beginning of class to reinforce their importance.

Typically, you will be leaving assignments that require students to copy some notes you have left behind or read quietly from their textbooks. They will then be asked to answer some questions or complete some other type of written assignment. They might even be asked to take a short quiz on the information.

Establish Emergency Lesson Plans

You should create a stock of emergency lesson plans in case you have to call in for a substitute at the last minute. These are usually left with the substitute coordinator in the office or with your fellow teachers. Make sure to leave the name of the person or people who have copies of your emergency lesson plans in your substitute folder.

Because you do not know when you will use them, emergency lesson plans will obviously not relate directly to what you are teaching at the time you will be out. Here are a few ideas for some plans you can create:

- Questions from a chapter in the book that you are not planning to cover
- Worksheets that are self-inclusive
- Teacher-created worksheets that might be considered interesting or fun, such as crossword puzzles
- Outside readings with questions

You don't know what your students will be scheduled to learn, so stick with general activities that will give the substitute something educational to do with the students.

141 Schedule Your Sub Yourself, If You Can

Every school and district has a different system for scheduling substitutes. Some schools even require teachers to call and arrange for their own substitutes through a centralized district substitute bank. Make sure to learn the steps you must go through when you first begin teaching. It may be too late when you wake up early in the morning and discover that you're sick and need a substitute teacher.

Despite all your efforts, there will be times when you will need to call in at the last minute to get a substitute. Most schools and districts have a cut-off time by which you need to call. Hopefully, you will have a nice person who is in charge of answering the phones in the morning and who remembers that you are calling in because you are sick.

However, if the person is not particularly nice or caring, do not allow yourself to feel guilty for doing what is in your best interest. Remember, they are probably stressed too. You should make sure to stay polite despite their actions. Keep things on a professional tone at all times. Remember, this person may be a huge help to you at some future point in your teaching career.

Inform Your Students

142

When you know you're going to be absent, you need to make sure that you inform your students. Go over your expectations for them in terms of work and behavior and reiterate that all work must be turned in to the substitute. It is also a good idea to tell your fellow teachers that you will be gone. That way they can help the substitute if there are problems.

It is important to double-check with the substitute coordinator before your day out and make sure that a substitute has actually been scheduled for your class. There is nothing worse than not getting a substitute. When this occurs, your students will usually be farmed out to your fellow teachers. This not only destroys your planned lessons but disrupts other teachers' lessons as well.

Finally, make sure that you have left your lesson plans and your substitute folder in full view on your desktop. And if you aren't confident the substitute will be able to find the folder or that it may go missing, leave the information with the teacher next door.

143 Insist on Good Behavior

Sometimes students who do not normally create problems in class will misbehave with substitutes. Therefore, it is very important that students understand you have high standards for their behavior. When you come back from your absence, make sure you do not ignore any behavioral problems that occurred while you were out.

Make Your Expectations Clear

You should hold your students to a higher standard when you are not there. When a substitute is in your classroom, you want him to have a great day. For one thing, if he is a quality substitute, you will want him to return another time. For another, students need to understand that being rude to anyone is wrong. Students should realize that they will be punished if they misbehave.

Discipline and Rewards

When you state your expectations, you should make it clear what the consequences of misbehavior will be. You could choose to have students serve detention or write letters of apology to the substitute teacher. On the flip side, you should also provide rewards for exceptional behavior. Do this often at the beginning of the year and then periodically as the year progresses as a means of reinforcement.

Tailor Your Expectations 144

Understand from the beginning that you will have wonderful substitutes in your class, and you will have terrible ones. It is important to inform your substitute coordinator or the central substitute office about exceptionally good substitutes as well as those who had problems.

You should expect your substitute to keep the class under control while implementing your lesson plan. However, sometimes you will find that the substitute placed in your class does not do one or both of these very well. She might have a real problem with classroom control. Or she might have been successful at making the students behave while failing to follow the lesson plan you provided.

It's understandable that many substitute teachers have problems with student behavior. However, there is a difference between minor misbehaviors and neglect. You should be really concerned if students come to class the next day and report behavior that could have led to student injury or simply indicates neglect on the part of the substitute teacher.

You will also find that some substitutes do not follow your lesson plans. Be very careful as you leave instructions to make things clear. Do not assume that your substitute knows what textbook your class is using. List the materials the substitute teacher should use, and leave reference copies if possible. Misunderstandings will occur and should be expected.

Part Nine

Be a Team Player Without Being Exploited

As a teacher, you spend practically all of your time interacting with people. The majority of this time is spent in front of a class. In fact, sometimes you will feel like you rarely get to speak with other adults. However, it is very important that you spend some time building relationships with your school's administration and staff. These are the people who can either help to make your days better or make them much more difficult to bear.

145 Find Your Place at Your New School

You are in a unique position as a new teacher. The other teachers and people around you will probably have different ideas and concerns about you as you come into the school setting. Some veteran teachers might see you as a threat because you represent new ideas. This will especially be the case if you come into a staff meeting the first day and start speaking up about the ideas you want to implement. You might have some great ideas, but it would be wise to use a little tact and judgment before speaking with authority before a group of veteran teachers.

Other teachers will see you as someone to help. They may even try to mold you to their vision of what a good teacher should be. Be careful whose vision you follow, and make sure that it is consistent with your own beliefs. Just because someone who has been teaching for twenty years has a strong opinion regarding how you should teach, this does not mean you have to take this opinion at face value.

Let Others Help—You're Not Alone

146

Some teachers will try very hard to help you. It is advisable to take any offered help because it will only make your life easier. For example, if a teacher offers to help you create a rubric for an upcoming assignment, do not turn it down. He may have years of experience to offer as well as some real insight into making this activity more successful.

Similarly, if there is a teacher on your staff who is considered to be very effective, do not be afraid to ask for advice. Most teachers will be more than happy to talk with you. When you get it, pay close attention. You might find insights that will help you accomplish your goal to be an effective teacher.

If you are struggling with a student or a situation, do not be afraid to ask the veteran teachers for help. This is not to say that you have to follow their advice, but if you gather many opinions about your situation, you will then have a bank of ideas from which to work.

147 Don't Take On Too Many Extra Duties

New teachers are often hoodwinked into getting involved in too many projects. They are new to the school and often enthusiastic about teaching. Veteran teachers are often overworked and involved in other projects, so they just do not have the time to participate in one more thing. Some people and schools are better than others at protecting their new teacher's time. However, more often than not, new teachers will be approached and asked to be a part of numerous activities. While participating in activities, committees, and projects is very important in helping you get to know the administration, other staff members, and students, you should try to avoid getting too involved during your first year.

Do not volunteer for every duty that comes along, but be smart and get involved with those that will give you the most reward for your time. This might sound mercenary, but you are the only person who will look out for your own best interest. Decide what you want out of your career and make your choices accordingly.

Get to Know the Right People

First and foremost, if you are a positive person who is committed to doing a good job, you will have a much easier time getting along with the people who are important in your career. When you build good relations with key people, you will find that they will bend over backward to help you out.

Administration

It goes without saying that throughout your teaching career you need to keep your bosses happy. They are the ones who control whether you will be hired each year. They are also responsible for dispersing teaching assignments, which can make your life easier or more difficult. The assistant principal directly in charge of you along with the principal of the school will have the greatest ability to influence decisions about your future.

Office and Support Staff

While the administration is important for the big decisions, the office and administrative staff are much more important on a day-to-day basis. People in the office who you need to make sure that you get to know include the bookkeeper, the substitute coordinator, and the principal's secretary. Other support staff members can also make your life much easier. Those you should try and build relationships with include the media center personnel, the technology coordinator, and your custodian.

149 Learn the Chain of Command

One of the first things that you should learn at a new school is your chain of command. Find out the name of your supervisor, their supervisor, and so on. Once you know this, you should follow it when you have issues.

You should discuss problems with your direct supervisor first. This gives your supervisor the opportunity to resolve your problem without sending it any further up the chain of command. If you do not allow your supervisor to try and resolve your issue, you are sending a message that you do not trust that he will do what is in your best interest.

If you go to your direct supervisor and she ignores your problem, then you have full rights to go to her supervisor. However, you should realize that when you do, you will probably cause some hard feelings with your supervisor. Make sure that the issue you are dealing with is truly an important one that justifies going further up the chain.

When Not to Follow the Chain

There are times that you should not follow the chain of command. For example, if you have an ethical issue with your direct supervisor, it only makes sense to go directly above him with the problem. Similarly, if each member of your administration has different focuses, you would go directly to the individual who is in charge of the area where you have a concern. Always use your common sense when you are dealing with issues and problems to guide you to the correct person for your situation.

Make Friends with Certain Teachers

Some colleagues you meet will be positive and inspiring—these are the types of teachers that you can learn from and aspire to. Let's take a look at two types of people you will want to get to know.

The "Excited" Teacher

The excited teacher is a great person to spend time with. She will often be positive about her job and will be involved in her school. However, you should be careful that these individuals do not get you too deeply involved in any projects when you are new to the school. They have often been teaching long enough to feel confident in the classroom and to have all of their lessons in place. It's fine to become friends, but do not allow yourself to be pushed into more than you can handle.

The "Committed Realist" Teacher

This individual is very committed to his job, yet he is realistic about the state of education and the school. While these individuals are sometimes seen as negative by administration, they often have the most stable view of what is really going on around you. Therefore, it is good for you to get to know someone like this to help ground you in reality. However, realize that this could have some negative connotations for you. Use your common sense to judge how committed teachers like this really are to providing an excellent education for their students.

151 Don't Let These Types of Colleagues Bring You Down!

Take care choosing the teachers with whom you have strong friendships, because like it or not you will be judged by the friends you keep. Following are some types of teachers that you might encounter as you teach.

The "Ready to Retire" Teacher

You should watch out for those "ready to retire" teachers who are unhappy with any changes that come their way. If a new change occurs, they may see it as more of a nuisance than an opportunity. This negative attitude is very catching and can deflate you very quickly.

The "Tenure" Teacher

Tenure teachers are those who may have a cavalier attitude about their careers. Often, tenure teachers are negative about any new or different ideas for education. If you hang around those teachers who have a negative attitude, this will rub off on you.

The "Incompetent" Teacher

This is the teacher who appears so incompetent that other educators doubt whether she can really teach. You will hear horror stories from other teachers and students about her classroom environment. If you really feel that something terrible is happening in a particular teacher's classroom, discuss this with your team leader and/or your immediate supervisor.

Stay Away from Staff Gossip

The school campus is a prime place for gossip, and you'll be exposed to it as well. Many times gossip is told over lunch or during planning periods. The best advice you can get as a new teacher is: "Listen, smile, and move on." In other words, if you do not want to be rude and say something like, "Please do not gossip in front of me," just listen to what is said without making any judgments at all. Some of what you hear will be true, and some will be false. As a new teacher, you may not have all the background information to make the distinction between the two.

It is in your best interest not to spread gossip around. For one thing, as a new teacher you will not really understand all the inner workings of the staff. There might be teachers who once dated or teachers who are related to each other. If you said the wrong piece of gossip to the wrong person, it could really cause a problem. It is best if you just don't get involved.

153 Learn to Deal with Personality Conflicts

The odds are that you'll eventually encounter a colleague with whom you just cannot seem to get along. This person might be another teacher with whom you have little contact. However, it might also be someone more important to you, like your team leader or supervisor. The best thing you can do in this situation is to try harder to get along, even if it seems like you are doing all of the bending.

This does not mean that you should always give in or that you have to be this person's best friend. But it does mean that you should be friendly and look for ways in which you can be helpful. With this attitude, your interpersonal relationship is likely to improve.

You might even find that you can build a good working relationship from a somewhat rocky start just by being the first to swallow your pride and move forward. Remember, your job and your time revolves around your attitude. If you approach each person and situation in a positive manner, you will have a much happier and enjoyable time as a teacher.

Start Off on the Right Foot and Get Involved!

Connecting with students can truly make the difference between being a success or a failure as a teacher. Even though it will require extra effort, there are many benefits to getting involved with extracurricular activities.

Meeting Other Educators

By participating in committees and extracurricular activities, you will be able to meet other teachers with whom you might not have had contact. Because of the solitary nature of teaching, it is often easy to stay isolated in your small space. However, meeting other teachers can have huge benefits for you. You might also get to know administrators and staff members better. Being involved with them in less formal ways can help you build enjoyable and fruitful relationships with them.

Getting to Know the Students

When you get involved with clubs, sports, and other extracurricular activities, you can really get to know students. This can help you in your own classroom as you build relationships and also in the school at large. For example, if you are on duty in the lunchroom and a student from another class begins misbehaving, you will have a better chance of handling the situation if you actually know the student or her friends.

155 Be a Team Player!

If you are seen as a team player, you will find that even though you are given extra duties and work, you will also be given greater consideration in the future. You will find that administrators will often work out ways to grant requests for teachers who are part of the team.

Being a team player also means that you will feel a greater sense of belonging to your school. If you feel that you are truly a part of the school, then being involved will have more appeal because you want your school to succeed in all endeavors. This does not mean that you should avoid having a personal life and devote all your time to your school. However, your attitude truly determines whether you see participation as a positive or negative experience.

Proving You Can Be Trusted

Keeping promises and showing that you are trustworthy is an important skill that you must nurture. Nothing can replace someone else's trust in your abilities and your word. Similarly, if you are not considered worthy of trust, you will find that many doors will be closed to you. Therefore, if you do become involved in something, give it your full attention. If this is not possible, go to your administrator and explain the situation. They will trust you more if you are honest with them than if you try to do something halfway and fail.

Embrace Your First Assignment

Before you even begin working at your new school, much of what you will experience your first year has already been decided for you. Administrators make course and teacher assignments over the summer. Because you are the newest addition to the school, you can expect that you will probably not be given the choicest assignments.

This does not mean that the administration is out to give you the hardest work. However, realize that many teachers feel that they should be given the better assignments because they have worked their way up the seniority ladder. Also, remember that they probably started out teaching the less than desirable assignments too.

One reason that new teachers do not always have the best luck with teaching assignments is because veteran teachers often have a say in what they are teaching each year. Many times administration will ask members of a department to get together and give them a guide to who will be teaching what the following year. Usually teachers will continue to teach the same subject each year. However, if someone who has a "choice assignment" leaves or retires, the most senior teacher who wants to change assignments will get their courses. What this means for you is that those individuals who had the worst teaching assignments will move out of them as soon as they can, leaving them for the newest person on the staff.

157 Learn from Leftover Challenges

Many new teachers are given all of the leftover courses. For example, a new high school social studies teacher might have the following schedule:

1. Planning Period
2. Economics
3. World History
4. Honors Economics
5. American History
6. Law Studies

You may think that a school should realize the obvious—that a new teacher has so many other issues to be concerned about, assigning her to teach five different subjects is just a recipe for disaster. However, the only way a school can remedy the situation is by forcibly moving veteran teachers who have been teaching their courses for a while out of their assignments.

Difficult Students

While this does not happen everywhere, in many schools across the country veteran teachers are able to influence who is and is not placed into their classrooms. As a result, your classes could have a higher percentage of troublemakers than others.

If you find that you have a large number of very difficult students in your classroom, do not be afraid to discuss this with your mentor and possibly your administrator. Sometimes administrators will separate students who have a hard time working with each other.

Participate in Committees

158

Most schools have committees that require teacher participation. Usually teachers have to be a part of at least one committee, so you will probably be assigned to or asked to join a committee during your first week of school or even earlier. If you are assigned to a committee, then you just have to deal with whatever committee is given to you. However, if you are allowed to choose, realize that not all committees require the same amount of work. If you can, try to pull aside a veteran teacher and ask their opinion about each committee's workload. You may find that the Testing Committee requires many hours of work while the Technology Committee does not.

Even with this information, you may not get the assignment you ask for. Many times there will be committees who need members, and you will be asked to join those. As a new teacher, it is often difficult—if not impossible—to say "no" because you are not on a permanent teaching contract. If you can, limit your committee membership to just one committee. In other words, you might not be able to say "no" to two committees if asked, but do not volunteer to join a second committee.

159 Figure Out Membership

You may find that other members turn to you with extra work. While it is expected that as a committee member you will fully participate, you should speak with your committee leader if you feel that you are given the majority of the work. If you are very agreeable to everything without ever speaking up, you will be taken advantage of. This is especially the case if you are not only agreeable but also efficient. People who are known as hard workers usually get the most work.

With all of this said, if you do have the time and the interest to get involved, then you can make a real reputation for yourself at your school. If you have a goal to become an administrator, then you might want to consider joining a committee that gets you noticed. Committees vary in all schools, but some are more prestigious than others. These are the ones that wield more power in the day-to-day running of the school.

160 Get Involved with Your Students in Extracurricular Activities!

Another issue you may face is being asked to participate in extracurricular activities. Realize that you will probably be "required" to participate in some fashion. However, be careful to limit the number of activities you volunteer for based on all your other involvements and obligations.

Sponsoring a Student Club

Most schools have a large number of clubs. Each year, new clubs arise and established clubs lose their adult sponsors. You can expect that you will be approached at some point to become involved with a school club. Some clubs are much more time-intensive than others so make sure to consider the amount of time required on your part before signing on.

Coaching a Sports Team

You might be asked to take part in your school's sports program. You might be asked to attend games to provide extra adult supervision, or you might be approached to actually coach a team. Being a coach of a team is often very time-consuming, depending on the sport you coach. Certain sports have shorter seasons and/or less student participation. However, coaching usually involves a supplement to your pay. If your goal is to someday be a coach of a major sport, you will definitely want to volunteer and become involved.

161 Do You Have More Duties Than Anyone Else?

As a new teacher, you may also be required to perform various duties around the school. For example, a "lunch duty" may require a teacher to sit out in the hallway or at a specified location to make sure that students at lunch do not disrupt other classes on campus. You might be asked to be a monitor of a tardy hall or a detention room. Some duties are more intense than others. Your school might ask for input before they assign the teacher duties so you might want to talk with your mentor or fellow teachers about the best and worst duty assignments.

If there are more duties than teachers to perform them, new teachers are often asked to fill in for extra duties. In most cases you will not be able to refuse these duties, especially if it's an administrator who's doing the asking. Therefore it is in your best interest to happily accept these extra duties because then you will be seen as a team player. Do not begin your first year of teaching by being seen as a complainer.

Say "No," Sometimes 162

As a new teacher, you will probably be asked to do more than is humanly possible. When you find yourself completely overloaded, it is extremely important that you say "no" to some of the activities presented to you. Declining to participate can be difficult, but it is a skill just like any other you will learn as you teach.

The first thing you should remember is to pick and choose wisely. If you wish to become involved in the running of the school, become involved in a greater number of committees and activities that affect the school itself. If you are more interested in building relationships with students, spend your time participating in clubs, sports, and extracurricular activities.

When you have determined that you cannot add any more to your plate, politely decline further invitations to participate in other activities. When you say "no," explain your reasons. List what you are already involved in and why you just do not feel that you can give the activity the time it deserves.

If you do not feel comfortable with a firm "no," you could offer your services in a limited capacity. You might offer to provide supervision or participate in one event. This shows the person involved that you are willing to help and be a team player.

In the end, you have to take care of yourself. Look at participation as an opportunity, but at the same time do not accept every invitation that is presented to you.

Part Ten

Recipes for Success: First Days and Beyond

As a new teacher, you can expect to spend more time just trying to survive than doing anything else. You will devote many hours trying to keep yourself organized and dealing with new situations as they occur. As a teacher, you will feel that you are being pulled in many directions. You will often be admired, pitied, and derided at the same time. You will find that everyone has expectations of what you should do and how you should teach. Remember what really matters is whether you feel good about the job you have done at the end of each day.

163 Foster an Effective Learning Environment

The effectiveness of your learning environment depends on you. If you create a roomful of distractions, you will probably have a lot of distracted students. However, if you create an atmosphere where learning is expected and rewarded, you will probably get many students who actually do learn in your classroom.

Organization Breeds Confidence

One of the biggest problems for new teachers is dealing with all the paperwork and minutiae of teaching. Many times, new teachers enter the classroom not realizing that they need systems for dealing with late work, tardies, absences, and taking attendance. Without a system of organization in your room, much time will be wasted dealing with mundane, housekeeping issues.

Using the advice given in this book, create your own system of organization for each of these issues. Decide before the first day how you are going to have students get their makeup work. Decide what you are going to do about late work. Spend some time up front to get organized, and you will be able to save much time later.

Remember that organizing does not stop with your room and your belongings. You should also have a well-thought-out discipline plan in place and ready to go. Students will try you during the first week of school. If you have a system in place, you will feel more confident as you deal with disruptions and other unexpected situations.

Make Education as Valuable as You Can

164

Education is important for so many reasons. It broadens horizons, making students more willing to be accepting and understanding. It gives students a sense of the past, allowing them to go forward with a basis for making decisions. It teaches students skills that will help them succeed in their lives after school. However, the ultimate goal of education should be to instill a desire to learn. Students should leave school armed with the tools to be able to continue their education on their own.

Realize that there is so much information available that no one can ever "know it all." In fact, you can expect your students to forget between 50 and 75 percent or more of what they learn in your class as soon as they leave it. This does not mean that teaching individual facts and having students memorize things is a waste of their time or yours.

Unless an individual knows some basic information, he will appear ignorant. Basic facts are also necessary in the scaffolding of new information. People learn new information and remember it for the long term by connecting it to already existing information in long-term memory. If there is a weakness in a child's educational past, this will become magnified as they move through school. It is a false belief that memorization holds no place in education. With that said, education should be much more than just lists of terms and concepts to memorize.

165 Commit to a Good Attitude Those First Couple of Days

You must enter your first week of school with a positive attitude and the desire to succeed. That first week can be very scary and nerve-wracking at times. However, realize that in just a few weeks you will have figured out much of the everyday tasks and will be able to truly focus on teaching effective lessons.

Staying Positive

Positive people are ones who succeed. They do not necessarily believe that everything is rosy. However, they do believe that even if bad things happen, in the end everything will work out okay. Have this attitude as you teach, and you will be well rewarded. When you feel that things are going pretty badly, it may help to remind yourself that this, too, will pass. You basically have two choices in life: let events "happen" to you, or actively participate in each event in your life. Positive people are proactive. They strive to make the best of every situation.

Clear Expectations

Start the year off right by letting students know your expectations for yourself and for them. As stated previously, tell your students that you know that they can learn and you expect them to put forth their best effort. Further, help them understand what they should expect from you. To earn their respect, act fairly and consistently at all times.

Learn to Enjoy Your Kids!

It is amazing that there are teachers who do not like young people. These teachers typically love their subjects, but consider students to be a necessary annoyance that comes along with the job. Thankfully, not many people like this stay in the teaching profession for long.

You will spend the majority of your time with your students. It is essential that you like them and, more importantly, like the people you hope they will become. The education profession is all about being positive. If you cannot look for the good in your students, then you should not be teaching.

Do not be afraid of the press that kids get today. If you read the local news, you might get a feeling that kids today are worse than in the past. This is just not true. Kids today are no better and no worse than they were years ago.

Youth culture may be different and sometimes hard to understand, but if you look back to when you were a child, you may have heard adults questioning the values of your peer group. The generation gap is a known phenomenon that spans back through history. Because students are just children looking to find their own way in life, their attitudes, likes, and dislikes may seem foreign to you. Remember though that just because something is different does not automatically make it bad.

167 It's Normal to Be Nervous

You will most probably experience some nervousness before and during your first day of school. There are two ways of dealing with nervousness. You can choose to dwell on it, or you can work through it to focus on the excitement of beginning a new challenge.

Look Beyond Yourself

Realize that your students are probably nervous too. By focusing on them and trying to make them feel more at ease, you will ease your own fears at the same time. Try to get to know a few students at a time in the moments before and after class.

Fake It

Your students have expectations the moment they walk into your classroom. They expect you to be in charge of the class. One way to fight nervousness is just to fake it. You can feel completely nervous on the inside, but on the outside exude calm.

Do not broadcast to your students that you are a new teacher. Emphasize your previous teaching experience, even if it was just as an intern. Students will look to your attitude about things and situations. If you overreact on the first day, this will be seen as a weakness and a sign of inexperience. If you take things in stride and show a sense of humor while remaining firm, you can have a successful class and quickly calm the butterflies in your stomach.

168 Get Settled Before the Students Arrive

You will most likely have a week or a few days of planning before the students actually arrive. Some of this time will be spent in meetings. However, much of this time will be spent alone in your room. Sometimes it can be overwhelming to think about all of the preparations you need to finish before students arrive. Spend some time creating a checklist of everything you wish to accomplish. Realize that it is much easier to get things done before the students arrive on their first day of class than after classes begin.

You should also spend a portion of your planning week getting to know the school staff and the teachers around you. Introduce yourself and let the teachers around you know that you are new to the school. Ask them for advice. Many times, teachers will share information that you will not receive from administration or others. Further, by building these relationships from the beginning, you can have people to turn to when problems arise.

169 Make It Through That First Day

The first day of school will most probably go by very quickly. You will be performing some standard housekeeping tasks and dealing with students entering and leaving your class at different times depending on their scheduling problems. Even though you will not get a lot done in terms of curriculum on that first day, you have the opportunity to set the stage for the rest of the year.

Begin Immediately

Begin your course on the first day. Try to finish your housekeeping duties quickly, leaving five or ten minutes to start your course. Have a mini-lesson planned or give a pretest. Hold a class discussion about expectations concerning your course. Discuss a current event that has a bearing on what your students will be learning. In other words, send kids the message that even though it might just be the first day, you mean business.

If you talk to students, you will find that they have teachers who make them work and teachers who allow them to goof off. These labels are placed on teachers from the first day. Worse still, they follow you from year to year. It is very hard—though not impossible—to change your reputation. It is an uphill battle to suddenly become a teacher who requires hard work when you have been lax in the past.

170 Learn Students' Names by Paying Close Attention!

Learning names can sometimes be a difficult prospect for new teachers. However, if you know a student's name, you have a better chance at connecting with them and also controlling their behavior. A great technique is to learn a few names right away and use them during your first class. This lets students see that you are quick and also that you care enough to learn who they are.

Each day, try to learn a few more names. It helps to take attendance out loud for at least a week and require students to raise their hands when called. Through this repetition, you will learn who they are.

Realize, however, that you will have times when you forget a student's name. This can occur if a student is very quiet or if a few individuals with similar names sit together in your room. One little strategy is to walk around the room passing out papers in the first two weeks of school. Typically, you will want students to retrieve their papers on their own. However, if you are having trouble remembering who a few students are, you can walk around and call out each name as listed on the paper. That way, you can see who looks up and reacts.

171 Think About Your Impact on Your Students

Your school is a part of your community, and there are a lot of expectations that the community places upon its teachers. Citizens expect teachers to provide students with an education that prepares them for the future. They look to schools to teach students appropriate behavior. They also expect teachers to ensure that all students learn the basics that will help them function in civic society.

Preparation for Work

Many community leaders feel that schools are not doing enough to prepare students for work What they want is for their employees to be able to read and write, perform basic mathematic calculations, and think critically.

Good Citizenship

Communities also expect schools to turn out good citizens. This means they expect you as a teacher to reinforce skills such as punctuality and honesty. Some community leaders also stress the importance of teaching students to get involved. The move toward greater community service reflects the growing concern that students should learn to care for their neighbors.

Work with Your Kids' Parents 172

Parents have many expectations for teachers, some of which are appropriate and some not. Parents should and do expect teachers to provide a quality education to their children. They also expect that you as the teacher will treat their children fairly and with dignity. Many parents wish to be involved or at the very least informed of their child's progress.

Parents expect their children to be learning valuable information each and every day. With the increase in high-stakes testing, parents also expect that the educational system will prepare them to pass these exams. When the press highlights students who do not know basic facts, such as the name of the first president of the United States, this harms educators and the state of education.

Parents also expect teachers to respect and care for their children. When teachers do not respect their students and fellow teachers, they set a bad example and bring down the reputation of the school. It is very difficult to learn in a hostile environment. Yet this happens each and every day.

Remember when you next look out over the children in your room that each of them has a parent or guardian who loves them. Remember to treat them as you would if their parents were actually sitting right next to them. This can help you become more considerate of your students and their needs.

173 Keep Those Lines of Communication Open

Parents expect to be informed when their children are struggling. Do your best to avoid a situation in which a student is set to fail or not graduate, and you have not discussed this with his parents. Remember, parents can be your best allies in getting students motivated. Parents who feel as though you have shirked your duty of informing them about important situations can cause real problems for you with your administration and district.

As stated previously, you should attempt to call your students and their parents often. Of course, some students require more attention than others. If nothing else, make sure that you contact the parents of these high-need children so that you can get them to help you create a positive educational experience for their children.

Inappropriate Parental Expectations

Most parents believe that education is very important to their children's future life. However, there are some parents who believe that teachers should take over raising their children. They take the attitude that while their children are at school, they are the school's problem.

The fact is that students whose parents are involved in their education have a greater chance of succeeding, but there is not much you as a teacher can do to alter parental expectations. The important thing is to set boundaries for yourself and do the best you can. Unfortunately, this situation happens more often than any teacher would like.

Work with Your Students for the Best Results

Students also have major expectations concerning you and their class. They expect you to be in control at all times. They expect fairness and consistency. They also expect that what you will be teaching is pertinent to their lives. Make sure that you strive to live up to your students' expectations as much as possible.

Keeping It Real

Education is about preparing students for their future. This does not mean that everything you teach is equally useful to know. You will find that your students will learn the most and become the most involved when they feel intimately affected by the information presented. Therefore, you should give some thought to explaining the significance and importance of each of the lessons you complete in class.

This does not mean that you should throw out all lessons that are not going to have direct bearings on your students' lives. Instead, what it means is that you need to make the connections for your students, especially if they are not obvious. For example, you could be teaching a lesson on isolationism before World War II and then make a comparison to the situation in world politics today.

175 Get the Administration on Your Side

Your school's administration will have expectations for you. Administrators will expect you to be professional at all times. If they believe that you have acted inappropriately, they will discuss this with you and possibly subject you to further disciplinary action. They also expect you to be a team player.

Administration will also expect you to keep your students under control. It is a fact that the teacher who gets a lot of parent and student complaints to administration will be seen as a poor teacher. Unfortunately, in some schools if you write too many discipline referrals, you will be seen as a person who does not have good classroom management skills. This may not make sense to you because you might see referrals as a tool toward behavior modification. However, because referrals are the highest level of punishment you can dole out, they should be used wisely. Make sure to be consistent and fair with discipline.

Administrators expect you to vary your instruction and make changes and adjustments for students with disabilities. They take IEPs very seriously (as they should) and expect you to make every effort to follow through on each modification. Further, they expect that you will accept all students in your class equally, no matter what their disability.

Whether you wish to believe it or not, your actions both inside and outside the school reflect on the school and all teachers. You will also be required to follow correct procedure for daily tasks. Teachers who try to bend the rules usually end up getting in trouble with their administration.

Manage Your Own Expectations

You will feel pressure to live up to everyone's expectations. However, they are not as important as setting and meeting expectations of your own. Many of your expectations should be the same as those from the community, parents, students, and the administration

Daily Goals

Each evening before you go to sleep or each morning when you wake up, write down a goal or two for the day. Your goals should be challenging, but they should also be very specific and realistic. For example, you might set a goal of getting a student who never speaks up during a class discussion to become involved. Or you might make a goal that you will begin class on time each period. The point of this exercise is that if you have goals, you have something to strive for. Your goals should be compatible with your expectations for yourself and your students. They should not, however, focus on something you cannot change.

Now Reach Higher!

Strive each day to be the teacher who someone will thank someday for truly affecting her life. Strive to be the teacher who helps light a spark for some students who have never enjoyed school in the past. In other words, set your expectations high. When you meet them, raise the bar.

177 Don't Forget to Watch Out for Personal Opportunities

You should stay aware of opportunities for growth. Choose activities that will help you develop as a teacher. Attend conferences with an eye toward finding fresh ideas and insights.

Many teachers have found that the steps to become nationally certified have proven to be a real growth opportunity to their career. Not only do many states provide monetary incentives for successfully completing this great program, but you will also reap other more intangible benefits. You will learn more about yourself as a teacher as you take a critical look at your practices.

You also may find that when you begin taking on a leadership role in your school, you will grow more as a teacher and a person. Followers allow things to happen to them. They often complain but rarely do anything productive to institute change. Good leaders, on the other hand, should be a source of strength and a proponent for necessary change. They spend time looking for solutions.

You do not have to be an administrator to be a leader. You can choose to lead through your classroom, through positions like team leading, serving as a department head, or chairing a committee. You can simply choose to lead through your attitude. If you are a tactful, positive, motivated hard worker, you can make a difference in your students' lives and in your school.

Create a Rewarding Career

Teaching is truly a rewarding career. In the United States, we are very privileged to provide our children with a free appropriate education. Truly effective teachers treat each student as if they have paid handsomely for their education, and they should get something worthwhile out of it.

It can often be hard, however, to find joy in the job of teaching. Sometimes days are filled with red tape and disruptions. Some students and parents will not respect you no matter what you do. People will make comments to you about how horrible it must be to be a teacher. Yet through it all, remember why you became a teacher: to positively affect the lives of children.

Celebrate Small Victories

Teachers need frequent celebrations. Every time that you have accomplished a written or unwritten goal is a cause for celebration. Take the time to truly enjoy your small victories. Treasure any words or notes of praise and pull them out when you need a pick-me-up. Spend time with fellow teachers discussing positive comments that you have heard students make. If you are spending all week just counting the days to the weekend, then you are not in the right job.

179 Taking Part in a Noble Profession

Teaching truly is a noble profession—ever-changing and always challenging. You can meet the challenges of teaching and succeed. It is an amazing thing when students come back to you after they have left your course and tell you how much you have meant to them. As Carl Jung said, "One looks back with appreciation to the brilliant teachers, but with gratitude to those who touched our human feelings. The curriculum is so much necessary raw material, but warmth is the vital element for the growing plant and for the soul of the child."

Much of being happy in life and in your profession is looking at the positives and working to eliminate the negatives. If you want to succeed, be positive in attitude and action. Do not look for trouble, because you will surely find it. Instead, look for inspiration, beauty, humor, and growth in yourself, your students, and your coworkers. Wherever you will focus, there will your heart be. So do not spend time focusing on the negatives of teaching. Instead, stay true to your beliefs about the value of people and of education.

Checklist for Your Room

- ❑ Create bulletin boards with an eye toward enhancing your curriculum without being distracting.
- ❑ Organize your room into separate areas devoted to specific tasks and resources.
- ❑ Place items where they make the most sense in terms of use such as placing your most used files in the cabinet closest to your desk.
- ❑ Take inventory and gather your supplies.
- ❑ Make sure you have a pencil sharpener, chalk, and erasers.

Checklist for Your Desk

- ❑ Your course's texts and books
- ❑ Your lesson plan book
- ❑ Your attendance book and sheets
- ❑ Hall passes and discipline referrals
- ❑ The substitute folder and information
- ❑ Post-It notes, paper clips, paper, pens, and pencils
- ❑ A stapler, tape, and a pair of scissors

180 Tips and Tricks

1. Face Your New Reality
2. Anticipate Your Students' Expectations
3. Learn the Ingredients for Success
4. Keep a Positive Attitude
5. Be Consistent
6. Make Sure to Follow Through
7. Learn to Be Fair
8. Start Each Day Fresh
9. Be Flexible
10. Keep Your Expectations High
11. Shed Those Biases
12. 9 Methods to Communicate Expectations
13. Learn How Students Respond to Goals
14. Accomplish Your Own Goals
15. Develop a Vision
16. Don't Be Afraid to Succeed!
17. If You Make a Mistake . . .
18. Develop a Teaching Style All Your Own
19. Get Your Rules Straight
20. Enforce Rules from Day One
21. Make Rules Apply to Everyone, Every Day
22. Make Do with Missing School Supplies
23. Develop a Tardiness Plan
24. Institute a Late-Work Policy
25. Make Students Make Up Work
26. Establish Rules for Restroom Visits
27. Be the Boss
28. Plan to Discipline
29. Enforce All Your Rules
30. Listen Actively
31. Try a Little Humor!
32. Be Specific When You Praise Students
33. Positively Reinforce the Right Way
34. Watch Out for Negative Reinforcement
35. Call the Parents When . . .
36. Get Results from Parent-Teacher Conferences
37. Set Up and Seat Your Kids
38. Decide about Your Desk
39. Take Time to Decorate
40. Stock Up on These Important Supplies
41. Take Textbook Distribution into Account
42. Offer Other Reading Material
43. Make a Plan for Your Paperwork
44. Organize with These Tricks of the Trade
45. Lean on Lesson Plans
46. Establish an Objective
47. Mark Your Calendar!
48. Work with State and National Standards
49. Learn to Handle High-Stakes Testing
50. Capture the Ideas that Are All Around You
51. Find Time for the Most Important Things
52. Make Homework Count
53. Let Your Kids Have a Life Outside School
54. Plan for Lesson Flexibility
55. Engage Your Students
56. Write in Journals Every Day
57. Stay on Top of Attendance
58. Collect Homework the Right Way
59. Repeat and Review Your Key Points
60. Organize and Discipline
61. Take Control of Your Time
62. Be Ready for Downtime
63. Get to Know the Three Learning Types
64. Cater to Your Kids' Styles
65. 9 Measures of Intelligence Revealed
66. Vary Your Skills for Better Overall Instruction

67. Lecture—Only Sometimes
68. Have Discussions in Groups—with Rules
69. Try Cooperative Learning Lessons
70. Teach Them How to Learn Together
71. Using Unique Lessons
72. Include All Students in the Lesson
73. Combat Prejudice in the Classroom
74. Stash Bad Thoughts Away
75. Deal with the Controversy
76. Teach and Learn by Debate
77. Recognize How Religion Fits
78. Find a Place for Politics Too
79. Guard Against School Violence
80. Beat Bullying
81. Expect (and Plan for) the Unexpected
82. Cope with Too Few Textbooks
83. Teach with No Textbooks—If You Have to
84. Deal with Outdated and Inaccurate Texts
85. Overcome Overcrowded Classrooms
86. Manage the Room Even When You Are Outnumbered
87. Tailor Lessons to a Large Class
88. Dispersing Kids When There Are Too Few Desks
89. Teach Different Level Classes—Multiple Preps
90. In Case of Emergency
91. Make Sure Your Assessments Are on Point
92. Pretest to Know Where to Start
93. Recognize What Grades Really Mean
94. Use Rubrics
95. Create Effective Rubrics
96. Find Time to Grade
97. Peer Grade/Edit—Helps Everyone Learn
98. Teach Academic Integrity—A Weighty Issue
99. Avoid and Deal with Plagiarism
100. Use the Internet to Your Advantage
101. Understand the Purpose of High-Stakes Testing
102. Get to Know the State of Education Today
103. Realize What's at Stake
104. Plan for High-Stakes Testing
105. Find What's Good about Standardized Tests
106. See What's Not Good about Standardized Tests
107. Know How the Tests Affect You
108. Teach to the Test?
109. Look at the Disparity Among School Funds
110. Make and Suggest Smart Purchases
111. Use Technology the Right Way
112. Make Lessons Better with Computers
113. Learn to Monitor Their Online Learning
114. Watch What and Who You Trust
115. Integrate Technology Effectively
116. Find Other Options If Your School Can't Afford Much
117. Determine How Valid Virtual Education Is
118. Look at a Case Study: The Florida Virtual School
119. Consider Online Learning—the Way of the Future?
120. Watch for Special Opportunities
121. Is Online Instruction for You?
122. Think about the Advantages
123. Realize the Issues for Online Teachers
124. Can You Handle the Commitment?
125. Catch Cheaters Even If You're Not There

126. Be Successful as an Online Instructor
127. Avoid Getting Sick
128. Take Preventative Measures
129. Be Your Own Substitute
130. If You Get Hurt on the Job
131. Recognize a Sick Building When You See One
132. Take Action to Fix Your Facility
133. Manage Stress on the Job
134. Don't Be Too Hard on Yourself
135. Gain Relief from Stress
136. Get Your Sleep
137. Give Substitutes a Fighting Chance
138. Make a "Substitute Folder"
139. Plan for Productivity
140. Establish Emergency Lesson Plans
141. Schedule Your Sub Yourself, If You Can
142. Inform Your Students
143. Insist on Good Behavior
144. Tailor Your Expectations
145. Find Your Place at Your New School
146. Let Others Help—You're Not Alone
147. Don't Take On Too Many Extra Duties
148. Get to Know the Right People
149. Learn the Chain of Command
150. Make Friends with Certain Teachers
151. Don't Let These Types of Colleagues Bring You Down!
152. Stay Away from Staff Gossip
153. Learn to Deal with Personality Conflicts
154. Start Off on the Right Foot and Get Involved!
155. Be a Team Player!
156. Embrace Your First Assignment
157. Learn from Leftover Challenges
158. Participate in Committees
159. Figure Out Membership
160. Get Involved with Your Students in Extracurricular Activities!
161. Do You Have More Duties Than Anyone Else?
162. Say "No," Sometimes
163. Foster an Effective Learning Environment
164. Make Education as Valuable as You Can
165. Commit to a Good Attitude Those First Couple of Days
166. Learn to Enjoy Your Kids!
167. It's Normal to Be Nervous
168. Get Settled Before the Students Arrive
169. Make It Through That First Day
170. Learn Students' Names by Paying Close Attention!
171. Think About Your Impact on Your Students
172. Work with Your Kids' Parents
173. Keep Those Lines of Communication Open
174. Work with Your Students for the Best Results
175. Get the Administration on Your Side
176. Manage Your Own Expectations
177. Don't Forget to Watch Out for Personal Opportunities
178. Create a Rewarding Career
179. Taking Part in a Noble Profession
180. Checklists to Live By